THE GREAT BETRAYAL

The Great Betrayal

ROD LIDDLE

CONSTABLE

CONSTABLE

First published in Great Britain in 2019 by Constable

3 5 7 9 10 8 6 4

A CIP catalogue record for this book
is available from the British Library.

ISBN: 978-1-47213-238-3 (hardback)

Typeset in Minion by Hewer Text UK Ltd, Edinburgh
Printed and bound in Great Britain by Clays Ltd, Elcograf S.p.A.

Papers used by Constable are from well-managed
forests and other responsible sources.

Constable
An imprint of
Little, Brown Book Group
Carmelite House
50 Victoria Embankment
London EC4Y 0DZ

An Hachette UK Company
www.hachette.co.uk

www.littlebrown.co.uk

For Emmeline Liddle

Contents

CONTENTS

'BETRAYAL IS THE ONLY TRUTH THAT STICKS'
Arthur Miller

1

THE GREAT BETRAYAL

At about five o clock in the morning of 24 June 2016, I was woken by a woman shrieking excitedly in my ear: 'We've done it, we've done it!'

Done what? I wondered dimly, dragging myself from a disquieting dream in which giant mechanical Michael Goves were terrorising the country, stamping people to death and firing bolts of electricity out of their rusted metal arms. Done what? Had sex? Surely not.

'We've won!' The voice came again. 'We're leaving the European Union!'

I immediately sat upright. Christ! I followed my wife lumberingly downstairs, where she'd been all night watching the referendum special on the BBC. As soon as I saw Dimbleby's face I knew she wasn't lying: he looked aghast. A pall of appalled outrage hung over the entire TV studio. Those pollsters were there, trying to explain to the public why they'd got it wrong again. Why do they still employ these jokers? They have all the psephological insight of a kohlrabi. One of those octopuses they use to predict World Cup winners would be more effective.

I made some coffee for us both and sat down in a state of mild euphoria for a while, until my wife said, shrugging her shoulders: 'They won't let it happen.'

I looked back at the TV screen, at the ranks of terribly transgressed BBC employees, at the utterly forlorn main party politicians giving their verdicts and already saying 'we must respect the result of the referendum, BUT . . .' And I nodded. 'No, they won't let it happen.'

Later that day I put up a one-line post on my Facebook page. 'Betcha we don't leave.' Oh, yes. The sad sweet pleasure of being proved right. I should have started this book right there and then, but part of me still clung to a faint hope that a clear majority verdict on the part of the British people would be honoured and acted upon, because that would be the right, democratic, thing to do. The politicians were mandated to extricate ourselves from the European Union – not bits of it, all of it. How, then, would they be able to renege on that mandate? I could envisage very clearly that they would renege upon it, but the question was how.

This book explains the how. It's the stuff I didn't foresee at the time, that glad bright morning when everything seemed rather good with the world: the process, the narrative, the chicanery, the bare-faced lies, the subversion of direct democracy by every possible unaccountable institution, the welter of propaganda from our neutral broadcasters, the staggering political ineptitude, the lack of will, the duplicity, that joker? He has all the psephological insight of a kohl-rabi. One of those octopuses they use to predict World Cup winners would be more effective.

I made some coffee for us both – me and the wife, not me and Peter Kellner – and sat down in a state of mild euphoria for a while, until my wife said, shrugging her shoulders: 'They won't let it happen.'

I looked back at the TV screen, at the ranks of terribly transgressed BBC employees, at the utterly forlorn main party politicians giving their verdicts and already saying 'we must respect the result of the referendum, BUT . . .' And I nodded. 'No, they won't let it happen.'

Later that day I put up a one-line post on my Facebook page. 'Betcha we don't leave.' Oh, yes. The sad sweet pleasure of being proved right. I should have started this book right there and then, but part of me still clung to a faint hope that a clear majority verdict on the part of the British people would be honoured and acted upon, because that would be the right, democratic, thing to do. The politicians were mandated to extricate ourselves from the European Union – not bits of it, all of it. How, then, would they be able to renege on that mandate? I could envisage very clearly that they would renege upon it, but the question was how.

This book explains the how. It's the stuff I didn't foresee at the time, that glad bright morning when everything seemed rather good with the world: the process, the narrative, the chicanery, the bare-faced lies, the subversion of direct democracy by every possible unaccountable institution, the welter of propaganda from our neutral broadcasters, the staggering political ineptitude, the lack of will, the duplicity, the betrayal. The betrayal. Because that is what it is, regardless of whether you are a leaver or remainer. A grotesque and unprecedented betrayal of the country by our parliament, a betrayal of that majority which voted in good faith, which trusted in democracy and perhaps never will do so again. The people voted to leave the European Union. We will not be leaving the European Union. At the very best we will be staying in it to all intents and purposes, except without voting rights. Headed towards this anomaly, some kind of 'deal' that makes us worse off than if we'd merely remained EU members.

The maths should have made it evident on that day, three years ago. Yes, the House of Commons was mandated to deliver Brexit. But it was more than six to one in favour of remain. Not only that, but of the parties represented in the House of Commons, only one – the tiny Democratic Unionist Party – was in favour of Brexit. The others were all, by a majority – a large majority in most cases – against. The Conservatives, Labour, the SNP, the Liberal Democrats, the Greens, Plaid Cymru. The same was true of the House of Lords and, still more crucially so, the rest of our liberal establishment – the people with the power, the influence, the money. But it was still a question of: how? The result was straightforward enough. Every area of England and Wales, except for London, voted to leave. How could the establishment work its way into a position where it could offer the pretence of delivering that mandate while actually not doing so? Through what tortuous manoeuvrings would it need to turn?

It began with a very swift change to the narrative. Within a day of the victory politicians and commentators had been talking about a 'hard Brexit' and a 'soft Brexit', whereas hitherto we had simply been talking about 'Brexit'. At first, a 'hard Brexit' was leaving with no deal at all – although that changed as time progressed. A 'soft Brexit', it became quickly apparent, would not be much of a Brexit at all and was utterly dependent upon the good will – ha – of the European Union. Another narrative, however, stayed basically the same, but increased in intensity, in fury. This had been seemingly the main plank of the remainer argument – that those who were in favour of leaving were firstly racists and xenophobes. The remainers conflated a distaste for the EU among leavers with a distaste for Europe, and a worry about unrestricted immigration with a dislike of foreigners – a woeful misrepresentation of the majority of the country. They were also stupid, these leavers – uneducated thickos. They were not wealth creators, they did not have degrees. They lived in awful places – Sunderland, Middlesbrough, Mansfield, Boston, Clacton and so on. They were underachievers. This trope played its part in allowing the MPs to renege upon the decision of the electorate. The allegations that leave voters were all racists enabled MPs, and Labour MPs in particular, to feel better about themselves for gainsaying the democratic will of the people – because the 'people' were bad. And if they were not bad, just dense.

This latter trope was of huge importance to the establishment as, within days of the referendum, the BBC and other news organisations scrabbled around trying to find people who had voted leave but now regretted the decision because they hadn't 'understood properly what it meant'. (They never tried to find people who had changed their minds in the other direction, although there were plenty.) Because these thick bastards hadn't understood what was really meant by Brexit, perhaps the kindest thing to do would be to let them have the vote again, so that they can get it right? A confirmatory vote, if you will. Or better still, hilariously, a 'People's Vote' – because the first one was won by troglo-dytes, not people. And as the Prime Minister struggled through her witless negotiations with the European Union, so this fugue for a people's vote grew – because the thickos hadn't understood how complex it all was, had they? And look – see how complex it is now, how labyrinthine? You hadn't bargained for this, had you? And yet all the way along it was not Brexit that was the problem but the govern-ment's handling of Brexit. But this stereotype, of the decrepit moron leave voter, was crucial to the cause of not delivering Brexit. They knew not what they had done, these poor deluded bastards. So another vote was needed, or maybe no vote – just stop the process in its tracks.

Labour MPs could convince themselves that in opposing Brexit they were doing the best for their constituencies, despite what their constituencies actually had to say about the business. Conservative MPs did the same. And so parliament began to follow the narrative of the soft Brexit, the nice Brexit, the Brexit that wasn't Brexit at all, some-thing that might be offered as a sop to the idiots but which actually kept us in the EU in all but name.

Oh, and the elderly. It was elderly people who voted leave. Destroying the future of the younger generation.

And their votes shouldn't really count because they'll all be dead soon – a familiar theme among that extremist tranche of absolutist remainers.

Never have so many blameless people in this country been held in such contempt, or been subject to such vilification, by an elite. A transgressed elite.

Another narrative. The vote was invalid. It was not 'binding' – despite the promise of the Prime Minister that it would indeed be binding and the absence on the polling cards anywhere of the word 'advisory'. Sheer chicanery. Only 52 per cent voted leave – a proper vote would have insisted upon a 60–40 majority. Would it? Why would it? Those were the rules – a simple majority sufficed. Everybody knew that when they went to the polls, remainers and leavers alike. A football match won one-nil has still been won – the opposition don't demand that it's not a win at all because the score wasn't five-nil.

The majority of people in the UK didn't vote leave – another wholly asinine objection from that rump of infuriated remainers. No, indeed, they didn't. But we have a habit, in this country, and in most democracies, of counting up the votes of PEOPLE WHO HAVE VOTED – not the ones who didn't. An odd arrangement, but there we are.

Or the vote was invalid because the leave campaign – always the leave campaign, never the remainers – told fibs. Well, heaven forefend. If we nullified elections every time a politician told a porkie, we wouldn't have a democracy at all.

But all this epic, disingenuous, non-sequitur shit, this flailing around in pursuit of a bunch of Aunt Sally arguments, helped to grease the wheels of the remain lobby and assuaged the MPs in their confected anguish over not, actually, respecting the vote at all. The voters thick, misled and racist and not even a true majority, the vote suspect.

So this book is an attempt to describe how that all happened, how Brexit was defeated – in part by people who always wanted it defeated and did not really care a jot about the aspirations of those who voted leave. But partly also by sheer staggering ineptitude. Because that stuff played its part, too. Not only the ineptitude of the Prime Minister, although that is probably worth a book by itself, but also of those who genuinely believed in Brexit and wished – or seemed to wish – to make it happen.

We are left, at time of writing, in a kind of limbo. Theresa May tried three times to get her deal through parliament and failed on each occasion. Her deal did not actually involve leaving the EU in a meaningful sense. She is now gone. But the same problem faces the incoming Prime Minister, that the mathematics of the House of Commons will not allow a no deal exit from the European Union (a point that has already been made very clear by MPs) and, given the make-up of the House of Commons, is more likely to insist upon a deal that is even less effective at extricating ourselves from the clutches of the EU: permanent membership of the customs union, for example. And always looming in the near distance the prospect of a second vote – but this time gerrymandered so we get it right. A choice between a disastrous deal and remaining, for example. The establishment will not make the same mistake again.

May's deal? Here's how Martin Howe QC, Chairman of Lawyers for Britain, saw it:

> If the deal goes through, the next day we will not have left the EU in anything but name. For at least 21 months of 'transition' – extendable up to four years – we will have to obey the EU's laws and rules, and be subject to the Commission and the ECJ as now. The big difference is that we will no longer have a vote or voice in the EU institutions. So no vote or veto against EU law changes which damage the City, or against the Commission's use of State Aid controls to suppress our competitiveness.

So it's that, or something worse, or nothing. Betcha we don't leave. It was said with sadness back then in June 2016. It's said today with real anger.

2

WHO VOTED LEAVE?

I voted to leave the European Union, but it was a close call. There were several remainer arguments that seemed to me to have a lot of force. The first and most obvious was the state of peace that had existed on our fractious and often violent continent for the past sixty years. Was this a consequence of the Common Market, the EEC and the EU? I did not quite buy the insistence from those who wanted to leave that mere trade deals would have sufficed to bring tranquillity to a continent in which the perpetually shifting states had been at war with one another, on and off, for the best part of a thousand years and, most destructively of course, in the last century.

I felt a cultural pull towards the mainland of Europe too, even if I thought that this was trumped, if you'll pardon the pun, by a cultural pull towards the USA, Canada, Australia and New Zealand and indeed our Commonwealth, for reasons both linguistic and historic.

I worried too about the future for British scientific research and development. Between 2007 and 2013 the UK received £8.8 billion from the EU in funding for research, development and innovation. It is true that each year the UK is a net contributor to the EU of £9 billion and so, according to leavers, we could henceforth spend that money we had saved on science and technology, if we chose to. It was that 'if we chose to' that worried me. I suspected we wouldn't choose to. Undemocratic it may well be, but there is a benefit to having crucial funding ring-fenced from the five-year British parliamentary cycle, when manifesto pledges insist that every last penny of available spare cash must be siphoned directly into the gaping, ravenous maw of the National Health Service (as indeed the Vote Leave campaign implied). I was interested, too, in the work being done at the Culham Centre for Fusion Energy, with the Joint European Taurus (JET), an attempt after all these failed years to produce almost unlimited clean energy from the process of nuclear fusion. We have led the world in this research, with substantial backing from the EU. Such expensive projects are necessarily collaborative and bounded by treaties (such as Euratom); would we still be able to afford the same resources if we left the EU? Would we have the same access to scientific institutions on the continental mainland? And would we have the far-sightedness to spend for the future? I had my doubts. A year after the referendum I visited JET and mentioned to its boss, Professor Ian Chapman, that 93 per cent of British scientists had voted remain. He looked utterly askance. 'Who the hell were the other seven per cent?'

So, there was that – and then the impact that leaving the EU might have on my own area, the north-east of England. From 2014 to 2020 the EU bunged the north-east more than half a billion quid, funnelled through the North East Local Enterprise Partnership. It is an area of the country that, like one or two others, has been starved of government cash and comes way down the list of priorities for incoming governments, even incoming Labour governments. Further, a lot of jobs in the north-east are dependent upon ready and immediate access to the EU markets – something in the region of 100,000, according to the (Newcastle) *Chronicle*. Added to which is the £1.1 billion of inward investment that has come from companies in EU member states. Would all this not be put at risk if we left? The counter-argument, of course, is that the EU has also cost an awful lot of jobs in the north-east as well, the most obvious being the 3,000 or so kicked out of work when the Redcar blast furnace and associated steel slab plants were shut down because, so the government insisted, under EU rules they could not be subsidised, which may well have been a convenient excuse.

And then there was Project Fear. Hell, it got to me too, the killer bees and locusts, death and destruction. What if Osborne and Carney and the CBI are right, and our homes will become worthless and we'll all be out of work? It was only the shrill hyperbole of these claims that made me smell a rat. But I did wonder if voting leave might be an extravagance that I could afford, being on a decent wage, but which might have a thoroughly nasty impact upon the very poorest of us.

These arguments, largely about money, seriously worried me, as I know they worried many others. For me, they were just about eclipsed by the arguments in favour of getting out.

Quite a few of my reasons for wishing to leave the EU could be classed as 'Lexit', that awful nonce word coined to describe those who had left-wing doubts about the EU. First and foremost of these is unrestrained immigration, unrestrained freedom of movement. I can see absolutely why a Conservative government would applaud the continued, untrammelled influx into our country of millions of low-paid workers from EU countries, for the short-term fillip it gives to the economy and the undoubted benefits it bestows upon British businesses. But for the life of me I cannot understand why the left wing would go along with this grotesque exploitation of labour: the means, as Marx had it, by which the rich get richer. I fully understand that EU migrants contribute more to the exchequer than they take out: that is not the point. I have no animus whatsoever against the hundreds of thousands of Poles, Slovaks, Czechs and Lithuanians labouring on building sites, serving you coffee, driving you around London in taxis, picking your Brussels sprouts, or acting as nannies to your privileged brats. Or worse, subcontracted out by big firms to a complex network of agencies and with the status, effectively, of slaves, even to the point of being denied their passports. But the squalid conditions in which they are often forced to live should shame us all. Here's a description, from the *Guardian* on 11 January 2005, of exactly what I mean, regarding Polish workers employed by a factory that supplied Sainsbury's:

> The house the Poles had been taken to, in an anonymously respectable cul-de-sac in a quiet Exeter suburb that forms part of the Labour minister Ben Bradshaw's constituency, was unremarkable outside. Inside there was no furniture, just mountains of rubbish, piles of syringes, soiled mattresses on the floor, and a terrible smell. They slept on the bare mattresses that night and were taken by the minivan to their 2–10pm shift the next day.
>
> Twenty Poles were in the house the night the Guardian visited, 10 of whom were sleeping there, three and four to a small room, with the other 10 in another small house nearby. It was after 11pm and they had just been driven back from their late shift putting Sainsbury's chicken portions on plastic trays at the state-of-the-art Lloyd Maunder meat factory near Tiverton.

Yet it is not just these workers being exploited, of course, horrible though that is on its own. The influx of extremely cheap foreign labour exerts a downward pressure on the wages of the very poorest of British workers, something confirmed by reports from both the House of Lords and Migration Watch. It could not but do so. Therefore in an already low-waged economy at the bottom end, British unskilled (and some semi-skilled) workers saw their wages reduced still further. 'Not by much', remainers would insist. But when you are low-waged in the first place, not much can be crucial.

There are also the associative problems of pressure on
infrastructure in such a crowded island, particularly housing. But that is not my principal complaint. I simply do not
wish to be part of a supranational organisation that treats
the most vulnerable of us as chattels. I think it disgusting.
The British left used to think the same, but two things have
happened to shift its perspective.

First, any opposition to immigration became conflated
with racism. People who railed against immigration of any
kind were castigated as racists and xenophobes – a continual screech from the remain supporters throughout the
campaign, 'vile and uneducated racists', culminating in
Diane Abbott's characteristically asinine observation that
people who intended voting leave want 'to see less foreign-
looking people on their streets'. You stupid, stupid, woman.

The second thing that has changed is that the Labour
Party has now cocked its hat towards the affluent liberal
middle class, especially in London, which quite likes its
basement kitchen excavations done at half the price, and
which cloaks economic self-interest in a supposed appre-
ciation of multiculturalism.

So immigration was an important factor, as it was for
many. But it didn't quite clinch it. For me the stuff that really
compelled me to vote leave was the nature of the EU and its
aspirations, and my belief that the nation state is a preferable
means of government – for us – to any other. I quite understand why my affection for the nation state is not entirely
mirrored on the other side of the North Sea, where national
boundaries change every few generations as the consequence of wars propagated largely by overweening, er,

nation states. Sure, I get that. I understand that if you have misgivings about the previous behaviour of your own nation state (Germany) or the military vulnerability of your own nation state (France) you may take a different view and quite like the idea of your nation state being subsumed in some pacific supranational organisation, as a kind of expensive sedative or palliative. So, too, those nation states that have been nation states for a comparatively brief length of time (Germany, Italy, Croatia, etc.) and those nation states that are fissiparous and held together by a fairly weak bond (Belgium, Italy, Spain). Or indeed those nation states that may have great antiquity but are too small to stake their claims individually in the world (Luxembourg, Malta). But these countries are not the UK. Our boundaries have not much shifted over the years and nor have we bullied other European countries in some fascistic, expansionist reflex. We have a successful history as a nation state dating back three hundred years and arguably longer: it seems to work for us.

But then there are my misgivings about the EU itself, no longer simply a trading bloc, but a political entity that seeks at every turn to extend its power over the sovereign nations within it. I have some reservations, for example, about a political and economic union with countries whose economic and political culture is markedly different to the rest – Greece, most obviously, invited into the EU without seemingly a thought as to how its fragile economy could be successfully co-opted and which, as we have seen, resulted in an economic catastrophe worsened by the EU's egregious bullying. And, for that matter, Turkey, even if the prospect of its membership has mercifully receded of late. Much of what the EU has done has been ill-conceived and witless; its single currency, half-baked and fragile, its Central Bank utterly incapable of providing stability in times of crisis. Its ludicrous plans for a military role, thus jeopardising the hugely successful NATO alliance (which, incidentally, required pooled sovereignty, but to a clear, specific and finite end). Where would such a force be deployed and how long would it take the member states that it *could* be deployed? As Lord (David) Owen put it, the EU is 'the weak nerve centre of a flabby semi-state, with almost defenceless frontiers, where humanitarian rhetoric masks spinelessness'.

But more even than this, as a clincher, is the EU's increasingly authoritarian bullying of member states on political issues. If ever you wanted proof of the German sociologist Robert Michels's 'Iron Law of Oligarchies', then the EU provides it. Michels, writing in 1911, was referring to the inbuilt tendency of complex organisations to become both bureaucratic and undemocratic, no matter how well-intentioned they may have been at the outset. Elect a government of which the EU disapproves, be it too far to the right or the left, and the unelected bureaucrats of the EU will threaten you with all kinds of sanctions, including fines, embargoes and the withholding of voting rights. In Poland, for example, the people of the country elected the Law and Justice party with a massive majority and entrusted them to enact the conservative and populist policies that they had promised in their manifesto. This included reforming the judicial system by ridding the courts of unelected communist-era judges who were inclined to block the new reformist agenda. The EU came down swiftly and severely: you will not do that, we will stop your money and take away your voting rights. 'We expected that our arguments would not convince the Commission – not because they are weak but because the Commission is acting in a political way and not as an institution charged with protecting respect for European law and treaties,' Deputy Justice Minister Łukasz Piebiak was quoted as saying by the PAP news agency.

Quite. Hungary, meanwhile, did not wish to take in vast numbers of migrants from outside of the EU, the consequence of German Chancellor Angela Merkel's hilarious '*wilkommen*' policy, which has caused havoc across the continent and to which most European people are deeply opposed, if the election results and opinion polls are to be believed. Much as with Poland, the EU invoked Article 7 of its constitution with a view to possibly depriving Hungary of some of its membership rights (although not *all* of its membership rights: with the EU it's 'you can check out when you want to, but you can never leave'). The Austrians were warned that if they elected a populist right-wing chancellor or government, it too would face censure. The left-leaning populist Five Star Movement in Italy has been bullied over its pledge for a universal basic income for the poor, given the country's fragile economy. Greece was bullied, mercilessly, over the policies proposed by the left-wing Syriza party to escape from its enormous debts (extremely lucrative debts, if you are a German banker).

You do not have to support the policies of any of these parties to understand that what the EU is doing is quite

wrong, and in the case of Poland outrageous. It is not for
the Council of Europe or the European Court of Justice or
even MEPs to decide upon a country's judicial policy.
Pro-EU politicians in this country long denied the EU's
yearning for greater political control over its member countries, its determination to see greater integration. They lied,
or were terminally deluded. It has been there all along, and
nor has it reached its peak.

There was other stuff rattling around inside my mind
when I went to vote. The EU's expense, its hideous bureaucracy, its inept organisation, its third-rate politicians, the
Common Agricultural Policy – a scandal – and its exclu-
sion from the market of Third World states that desperately need to flog their exports. There were also more
questionable, attenuated reasons for voting leave, those
not based on a rational evaluation of the European Union,
but more visceral. A dislike and mistrust of our liberal
establishment, which adored the EU, for a start. A vague
and inchoate hope that this referendum might offer the
chance for those 'left behind', as we politely call the working class these days, to stick it to their ineffably smug
betters. And even schadenfreude, the pleasure to be taken
in listening to their screams of outrage on 24 June, the
temper fits and the tantrums. And schadenfreude towards
the likes of Jean-Claude Juncker: I do not think that the
UK should be told what to do by a regularly half-cut
superannuated Luxembourgish bureaucrat who couldn't
even make a decent fist of running his own microscopic
satrapy. Those were the less noble reason for voting leave.
But it should be said that they were not prominent in my

mind on 23 June 2016, because I did not think that leave would win.

Anyway, that's a very brief synopsis of why I voted leave. In short, I did not vote leave because I think Wogland begins at Calais and I don't want Brussels telling us what shape our bananas should be. You know?

I suspect it was much the same for the vast majority of those 17.4 million people who trooped down to the ballot box on 23 June: they made an evaluation, a careful judgement, and later discovered that, just like me, they were uneducated, stupid, racist and – worst of all perhaps – old.

There has been a multitude of explanations put forward to explain why a majority of the electorate voted to leave the European Union, occasioned, one supposes, by the shock that they did so. This is what we always do with politics: try to compress an enormously diverse and complex phenomenon into a kind of single, easily swallowable explanation. It is almost always wrong, and it is certainly wrong as far as Brexit is concerned. Were the leave voters uneducated? Well, not the 32 per cent of them who had university degrees, for a start, and without whom leave would not have won. Yes, a greater proportion of people with degrees voted remain. But to what extent is that a function of the affluence that inevitably attends to a university education, rather than the learning itself? And when you dig a little further down into the education statistics, apparent anomalies begin to crop up. So, a study by the London School of Economics in 2017 concluded that while there was a negative correlation between educational achievement and voting leave: 'Our findings, however, reject the dichotomous view of the low-educated Brexiter vs the high-educated remainer, by showing that two groups with *intermediate* levels of education (voters with good GCSEs and A-levels) were more pro-leave than the low-educated (those with no formal education and with low GCSE grades).' So was it the really, really, thick who voted remain, then?

It is true, too, that the most well-off people in the country, those in the AB sociological category, voted by a majority to remain. But by a fairly thin majority; again, without the 46 per cent of ABs who voted leave, leave would not have won. And then the familiar charge. The leave vote comprised the elderly, who spitefully denied the younger generation their future. Really? It is true that the younger you are, the more likely you were to vote remain. But one in four eighteen to twenty-four-year-olds voted leave and more than 40 per cent of twenty-five to thirty-four-year-olds voted leave, while much more than one in three seventy-five-year-old plus voters chose remain. The facts do not quite accord with the rather glib assessments made in the wake of the referendum. Without the young leave vote, leave would not have won. Without the educated leave vote, leave would not have won. Without the affluent leave vote, leave would not have won.

Was it that mysterious community, the 'left behinds', who won it for leave? It depends on what you mean by left behind. I do not feel terribly left behind. Nor, again, does the sociological breakdown entirely support that thesis. What about immigrants and the children of immigrants? Heavily for remain in the first category – rather less so in the second. A Bangladeshi friend of mine, who voted remain, reported that his Bangladeshi friends were split on the issue; the more integrated and – as he put it – 'pro-British' they were, the more likely they were to vote leave.

It is never quite so simple as the left-leaning social scientists wish to make it. The only definite conclusion we can reach is that 17.4 million British citizens voted to leave because they did not much like the European Union, and may have had a vast array of reasons for arriving at that conclusion. Are there other things that unite them, then?

Possibly. The closest explanation I have seen comes in David Goodhart's book *The Road to Somewhere: The Populist Revolt and the Future of Politics.* It's a good book. Put crudely, Goodhart suggests that the divide in our society, most clearly seen in the Brexit vote, is between two groups of people: the somewheres and the anywheres. Somewheres are rooted to their communities and feel a sense of place and belonging; as a corollary they tend to have an affection for tradition, history and nation state. Anywheres don't buy any of that stuff. They are rootless, unencumbered by either history or, for that matter, the present.

By coincidence, as Goodhart was finishing the writing of this book in 2016, I had a similar suspicion of what divided us, essentially, as citizens. I had just attended a reunion of my schoolmates from the comprehensive school in Guisborough, just south of Middlesbrough, where there was lots of alcohol and very happy – in the main – memories. It was forty years since we had left the school and a laudable hundred or so turned up – it was a large comp we had attended. The reunion was held a couple of weeks after the referendum and I asked as many of my old classmates as I could how they had voted. The answers were remarkable. Almost without exception, everyone who had left Teesside and made lives for themselves elsewhere, never coming back, had voted remain. And all those who had stayed on Teesside had voted leave. The more interesting point was that this was true no matter the educational achievements of the individual or how much money he or she was earning. The people who'd left and never returned, even if they'd suffered miserable and impecunious lives, were still for remain. The people who had stayed were for leave even if they had degrees from a good university and had made a fortune. There was something more intrinsic than social class, education, wealth or status going on. It was a state of mind. Goodhart explains it very well.

So that may get us somewhere towards the point. Whatever, it seems fairly clear to me that the people who voted leave were not a homogenous morass of elderly racist Little Englander thickos. And yet that is the accusation that was levelled at the leave voters during the campaign and has been both the text and the subtext of every argument against leave ever since. It began as a fusillade of insults – thick, racist, old – and has ended as a mediated version of that misapprehension. Listen, we understand you voted to leave, bless you. But you really didn't understand what you were voting for, did you? If you'd known, you would have voted remain, wouldn't you? But you were – oh, let's not be rude, let's say *misled by those awful people.* Not terribly bright of you, but we'll pass over that for the moment. Of course *we* knew right from the beginning: when we say, as we're campaigning for a second vote, *we* didn't know how it would work out we didn't actually mean *we*. We knew, you see. We meant *you. You didn't know.* It's just taken you a little while to catch up. And so we should either drop Brexit entirely or have another vote. What do you think? And this time would you try to get it right? Little cross in a little box. It's not *that* hard.

Such was the trope, these last two years: you're thick or you're credulous, both of which amount to the same thing. The contempt of some sections of the remain vote has been signal: a genuine loathing for those who think differently to themselves. And I suspect, as a theme, about as successful with its target audience as it was during the campaign. Sheesh, and they call us stupid.

Or maybe not just stupid, but stupid and almost dead. Or perhaps entirely dead. David Aaronovitch was the first mainstream media monkey to come out with the obnoxious observation that most of the winning margin of leave voters had died by now so if we held a second referendum remain would win. Obnoxious and pig ignorant. People's views change as they grow older. It's the old argument about the *Daily Telegraph* – how can it possibly survive when its readership is at death's door? Because people grow up to replace the dead. People who have suddenly recognised that they may have been mistaken, in the past. Not David, obvs. He's still trapped in his bubble. His very big bubble.

3

THE DEBATE

Perhaps the two sides of our divided nation can agree on one thing, at least. The debate about whether we should leave the EU or stay in it was characterised by crass disinformation, downright lies, absurd hyperbole, scaremongering and intense stupidity. On both sides. It is not entirely unknown for politicians to be less than truthful during election campaigns but on this occasion they really excelled themselves. A properly informed debate did not happen. That point I would cede to the remainers – but the notion that egregious shite was flung about solely by the two leave campaigns is typically one-eyed and, frankly, absurd. The remain campaign was, if anything, even worse in its disingenuousness and certainly less effective in its persuasiveness.

Campaigning began in earnest in April 2017 and the very good news for leave supporters was that the official remain campaign – Britain Stronger in Europe – had as its executive director the reliably useless Will Straw, son of the former Labour Foreign Secretary, Jack Straw. Will had been the Labour candidate for the swing seat of Rossendale and Darwen in the 2015 general election, a seat he had been predicted to win but instead managed to lose by a fairly convincing margin. His previous brush with notoriety had been to be booted off as governor of a failing school in Lambeth, London, a post that I'm sure he took very seriously despite living some distance from the school itself, i.e. in the USA. The former executive chairman of Marks & Spencer, and a Conservative life peer, Stuart Rose, chaired the campaign. It was basically a Blairite–Cameroonie coalition, personified by the ludicrous Roland 'Rat' Rudd, a PR executive, brother to the Conservative politician Amber Rudd and a former advisor to Tony Blair. Craig Oliver, a former BBC middle manager and previously David Cameron's director of communications, ran the, er, 'strategy'. A few fairly competent politicians from beyond the Blair–Cameron alliance also sat on the board, such as the Green MP Caroline Lucas and the Liberal Democrat, Danny Alexander.

Britain Stronger in Europe concentrated almost exclusively on money, how much we would lose, financially, if we were to leave the EU. Almost certainly a mistake, given the mindset of the general public. The disingenuity about money began in its first article published on its website, which offered, in tortuous syntax, 'six reasons you need to vote Remain on June 23rd'. Point Six asserted: 'For every £1 we put into Europe, we get almost £10 back.' This bizarre statement implied that somehow the EU gave us this money, when of course we are net contributors to the EU budget by a margin of about nine billion quid. It may well be that this is money well spent, although I have my doubts. But that stark statement of getting £10 back for every £1 put in was true only if you conflated membership of the EU with every single bit of business done with companies in EU countries: it was nothing to do with the EU itself. Britain Stronger in Europe always conflated the EU with Europe, as you can see from its name – as if in leaving the EU we would some-how be physically transported from Europe itself, perhaps to Africa. Already the bar had been set very low, then.

But it was the Project Fear (a term coined by Boris Johnson) stuff that really stretched the credulity – and in its hyperbole and rank inaccuracy surely rebounded on the remain campaign. The most wayward, or hilarious, of these came with the Chancellor of the Exchequer George Osborne's 'HM Treasury Analysis: The Long Term Economic Impacts of EU Membership and the Alternatives'. Never mind the long-term stuff. Osborne got straight down to the detail of what would happen not when we left the European Union, but immediately after we had simply *voted* to leave the European Union. Osborne's calm and rational analysis predicted that the UK would fall into 'immediate recession'. He continued: 'unemployment would increase by around 500,000 with all regions experi-encing a rise in the number of people out of work'. George felt able to be very specific about all of this, insisting that 24,000 jobs would be lost in Wales and 43,000 in Scotland. Meanwhile, house prices would fall precipitously. Instead, what happened in the two years that followed the vote? More than half a million new jobs have been created and unemployment is at a forty-six-year low. Employment is higher than it has ever been. There was not even the whiff of a recession; indeed, the economy edged upward, buoyed by new inward investment and a sharp rise in exports fuelled by a devalued pound. Even wages, for too long lagging behind inflation, began to perk up in 2018. Musing on the former Chancellor's ludicrous and arguably criminal predictions a year or so after the vote, the economist Tim Congdon, writing in the magazine *Standpoint*, called Osborne's analysis 'a giant error' and a 'gross miscarriage of government'. He continued: 'Instead of employment falling by hundreds of thousands, it has risen by hundreds of thousands. Instead of house prices going down, they have gone up. Instead of the public finances lurching more heavily into deficit, they have been better than at any time since the Great Recession, making the prospect of an eventual surplus far from silly.'

Congdon added that the campaign's errors were down to 'a mixture of malice and ignorance, of wicked politics and trashy economics. As usual with other policy blunders in recent decades, it was more cock-up than conspiracy'. Not so sure about that last verdict.

Having resigned as Chancellor, Osborne was suddenly and surprisingly offered the role of editor of the *London Evening Standard*, in some kind of genial *Jim'll Fix It* gig on the part of the freesheet's proprietors. From this podium he has continued to publish whole rafts of scary bollocks about what will happen when we leave the EU, my personal favourite being that we would all be ravaged by incurable gonorrhoea as a consequence of Brexit. Never mind gonorrhoea. Given the demented nature of both George's Treasury 'analysis' and the weird Brexit scare stories that he churned out at the *Standard*, it is tempting to suggest that Osborne had become deranged in the mind as the consequence of late-stage syphilis.

But he was far from alone in making stupid and alarmist predictions based on inaccuracies or downright lies. The formerly Conservative MP Anna Soubry, a remainer zealot who now sits as leader of the rapidly dwindling ChangeUK group of MPs, insisted that UK trade would fall to 'zero'. Not just drop a bit – there would instead be no trade whatsoever. Perhaps she meant it in a colloquial sense. Or perhaps she meant it literally. With Soubry, there's simply no knowing. Then there's David Cameron, the most prominent remain politician (as Prime Minister), who told a special referendum edition of the BBC's *Question Time* programme that the Islamic State (ISIS) were yearning for a leave victory in the UK. He also repeated his Chancellor's comments about recession and asserted that as a consequence the government would be required to hold a 'punishment budget' with cuts to public spending and higher taxes. Nope, didn't happen, wasn't needed. Earlier, Cameron had suggested that a vote for Brexit risked leading the UK into war. Dave, Dave. It doesn't really, does it?

One of the largest donors to the remain campaign was everybody's favourite banker, Goldman Sachs, which bunged half a million quid into the campaign – as well as the benefit of its expert advice. The UK would go into recession in early 2017, the firm declared, while Credit Suisse suggested there would be a 1 per cent fall in GDP. And as the *Spectator* reported: 'Days after the EU referendum, investment company JP Morgan announced in an email to clients that they expected Scotland to leave the union and change currency. (As did Andrew Marr in the immediate aftermath of the vote.)' As you may have noticed, Scotland has not left the UK and if the opinion polls are anything to go by, independence is further distant now than it has been for a decade. And it is still happily trading in pounds, so far as I am aware.

This was the tenor of the remain campaign. Hammer them with terrifying stuff about what will happen to the economy, even if you have to make it up yourself. And then, as a corollary, imply that those who are voting for Brexit are thick and probably racist. It is a strange way to go about courting the people you want to vote for you, telling them they are thick. It didn't work during the referendum campaign and it hasn't worked terribly well since, either. It is surprising to me that Britain Stronger in Europe has escaped the flak for what was, from start to finish, a misjudged and misleading campaign. It was, after all, the remain voters who felt let down by it. Matt Kelly is one of the country's more staunch remainers and editor of the (surprisingly good) anti-Brexit newspaper, *New European*. I asked him what he thought about the remain campaign. Was it any good? 'Well, if you set out to fuck it up at every stage, it was a magnificent triumph.'

There were two leave campaigns. Vote Leave was the official campaign, as designated by the Electoral Commission, and fronted by Boris Johnson, Michael Gove and the Labour MP Gisela Stuart. Its strategy was devised by

Dominic Cummings, a former aide to Gove and a man known for a certain irascibility, a knack for making enemies. Chief Executive was the political campaigner Matthew Elliott, a former boss of the right-wing TaxPayers' Alliance. Leave.EU, meanwhile, had its roots in UKIP and had been set up by Arron Banks, UKIP's biggest donor, and the entrepreneur Richard Tice. Banks had also wanted official designation from the Electoral Commission and had pleaded with Vote Leave for a merger and a joint campaign. Banks thought that two rival Eurosceptic campaigns would damage the vote. My suspicion is that he could not have been more wrong, an opinion shared by, among others, Nigel Farage. This double-pronged attack was hugely useful to the leave vote. It allowed the official Vote Leave campaign to focus on the gentler issues of the referendum, and concentrate its efforts on big cities, untouched by the supposed toxicity of Leave.EU, which majored on the more controversial issue of immigration and targeted smaller towns and the shires. Relations between the two campaigns were a little short of cordial, with Leave.EU being banned from attending the Conservative Party conference and petty squabbles over who should appear on television programmes. But the bifurcation worked. Every time Nigel Farage addressed the issue of immigration, such as standing in front of a giant poster on a bus showing thousands of what looked like Muslims pouring in to the country, under the heading 'Breaking Point', Boris and the rest of them could put their noses in the air and say: 'Nothing to do with us, guv.' And yet immigration was an important issue during the referendum, and justifiably so.

Vote Leave preferred to talk turkey about the money, but also to talk – somewhat strangely – about Turkey. On both issues they ran into controversy and the one that got the remainers really angry was the advert splashed against the side of their campaign bus: 'We send the EU £350m a week. Let's fund our NHS instead.' This is the most frequently raised example of misinformation from the leave camp and has led to a private prosecution against Boris Johnson for 'abuse of public trust'. (Yes, for standing in front of a bus with a stupid slogan on it). It is a strange thing for the remainers to have got themselves worked up about, even if the figure of £350 million seems to have been plucked from thin air and has no basis whatsoever in fact. The UK pays the EU approximately £13 billion per year, which translates to £250 million per week. But that is before you take into account the £4.1 billion we receive back in public sector receipts, leaving a net contribution of about £9 billion, or approximately £175 million per week. Either way, the £350 million was a gross distortion.

'A grave, grave error,' Nigel Farage told me (with just a hint of jubilation). 'I sat down with Michael Gove and said this is crackers – you could have just said £50 million or something. Gove said it's too late to change it now.'

Vote Leave was campaigning in big city centres where the NHS is perhaps the most pressing issue on the agenda, and the remain lobby was thus enraged at the apparently deliberate inaccuracy. But would one poster have swayed that many votes? It came close to swaying mine, I must admit. If I had thought for a single nanosecond that all the money we saved from not having to pay into the EU, however much it was, would be hypothecated directly to the NHS, I'd have voted remain. But still, wrong it undoubtedly was. Ironically, a year later the government announced an increase in spending for the NHS – of, yes, £350 million per week.

Vote Leave's next great weapon was to wave Turkey about in a vaguely threatening manner, suggesting that the country would one day soon be a member state of the EU and would you wish to join a club with *them* in it? Well, frankly, no, I wouldn't. But the threat was a little bit speculative and, what's more, dated. Turkey has been trying to negotiate its accession to the European Union since 1987 and things had been progressing smoothly up until about 2014. Back in 2010 our then Prime Minister, David Cameron, had visited Ankara and told his hosts that he was angered at the lack of progress in Turkey's negotiations with the EU and that the UK 'strongly supported' Turkey's membership. But that was four years before Turkey elected the appalling Recep Tayyip Erdoğan as President. Since the accession of this Islamist authoritarian, the EU has gone very cold on the idea of Turkey being a member state and, indeed, Turkey itself seems less keen on the notion too. Still, the prospect is, hypothetically, on the table even if the EU has stopped looking at the table and certainly won't be sitting around it any time soon. But would this strange obsession with the Turks have proved the difference between winning and losing for leave? I have my doubts that a single vote would have been cast on the issue, apart from maybe by some Kurds up in London N2. But misleading, as a campaign issue? Undoubtedly.

Leave.UK, meanwhile, did not tell any deliberate pork-
ies, so far as I can see. Farage's bus did seem to show lots of
people who didn't look very European queuing up to get
into our country, for sure. But this is surely a matter of taste
rather than accuracy. It is true that the majority of immigration into the UK is nothing whatsoever to do with
Europe: it comes from the Indian sub-continent, and would
continue to do so long after we left, unless the government
took action. But it is also true that Angela Merkel's decision
to welcome every single refugee from the Levant, the
Maghreb, the Sahel and so on into Europe had worried
many British (and indeed German, Czech, French,
Hungarian, etc.) people. The BBC and liberals may wreathe
themselves in concern for economic migrants from Asia
and Africa, but their untrammelled arrival into a defenceless continent is now seen as one of the more catastrophic
political experiments the EU has undertaken, and even
Merkel has now disowned the policy. Immigration was a
perfectly legitimate campaign issue and for many people
the most important: our need to control our own borders.

It was not a dignified campaign, on either side. Both
sides have received fines for being a little cavalier with their
spending. Neither side did much to elevate the debate. It
was at the time a moronic shriek-fest. It may well be that
the grotesque inaccuracies spewed out by George Osborne
et al. convinced a few people to vote remain. But to suggest,
as some remainers do, that the faults were all, or even
primarily, on one side is simply untrue. Yes, we were lied to,
repeatedly. Whodathunk it?

4

I DON'T KNOW ANYONE
WHO VOTED LEAVE

The howling began immediately. The howling began immediately and it did not stop. The howling is still with us, even now. A strange noise to the ears – a din of infantile rage, of transgressed hauteur, of absolutist fury, of a weird kind of totalitarianism, a kind of fascistic acid reflux. All occasioned by appalled shock. It came from that section of those who voted remain – not all of the remain voters by some margin, probably nowhere near a majority – who were simply unable to accept the result, perhaps because it had never occurred to them that their opinions could possibly be in the minority. Could ever be gainsaid.

My wife, picking up our daughter from school on the first Monday after the vote, overheard some other mother exclaim, almost in tears, to her friend: 'I don't know anyone who voted leave!' As if the vote had been somehow rigged. My wife butted in, probably a little rudely. 'I voted leave, actually.' And the woman turned to her, eyes wide with contempt and frankly horror, and said: 'How *could* you? You've got *children.*' We laughed about that response for days until we cottoned on that the initial statement – I don't know anyone who voted leave – would become utterly ubiquitous and was an expression of the great divide in our society. It would eventually help to strangle Brexit. I don't know anyone who voted leave, and therefore the poll was clearly invalid. I don't know anyone who voted Brexit and therefore nobody did, or nobody of consequence.

Then, the mass of defriendings on social media sites of those who had voted leave by those who had voted remain. So, for those who did know someone who had voted leave, albeit only through the stunted prism of cyberspace, the best recourse was not to know them any longer. To wrap themselves still further in their comfort blankets of uniformity of opinion. An opinion poll by YouGov in 2019 suggested that 37 per cent of remain voters had defriended, on social media sites, people who have voted leave (as compared with 9 per cent of leavers defriending remainers). That is an extraordinarily high percentage. Oddly it was only once leave had won that these defriendings took place: we were presumably thick, elderly neo-Nazis before the vote, but then that didn't matter so much.

The tweets of despair and anguish.

'In shock . . . the blackest of news . . . spent most of yesterday crying, couldn't get out of bed . . .'

'In a hotel room watching this s***t I feel very alone. Texting people I love telling them we'll be OK.'

Beyond parody, I know. And yet this stuff played its part in Brexit's inevitable defeat.

People kicked out of book clubs when it was revealed they'd voted leave. The howling, the long howling of the slebs – or, if you prefer it, the 'creative community'. Cumberbatch and that over-remunerated crisp-flogging dimbo Lineker. The parade of keening luvvies. The actor Sam West shaking his head and saying, 'Many people are in mourning.' An estimated 96 per cent of the acting community were for remain. The journalist Simon Jenkins, himself a remainer, wrote: 'London's creatives might have done better to stop for a moment and ask why Brexit showed provincial Britain to be so at odds with the capital. Could it be resentment at London's elite being so besotted with the glamour of abroad as to ignore its domestic hinterland? Could it be resentment at London's snout being so deep in the public-spending trough?'

But the fugue continued, online and on the BBC. Another remainer, Libby Purves, commented in *The Times*: 'Ashamed. Terrified. Shocked. Horrified.' But Purves said that it wasn't the actual vote that shocked her, but the 'online squawk' of reaction from cultural icons, colleagues and friends. The 'carry-on was beyond parody: anguished bunker-mentality tinged with patronising, generalising hauteur about those who voted Leave'.

Many threatened to leave the country, feeling suddenly alienated and averse. A couple we knew in Kent were in an apoplectic rage and announced that they were moving to Sweden. In the end they moved seven and a half miles down the road to Benenden, which is not quite the same thing, but still. Some really did get the hell out. The *Guardian* did a report on a whole bunch of them, including Pip Batty (crazy name, crazy gal) who was once a communications consultant but is now teaching English in Tbilisi, Georgia. 'There are people I don't speak to any more because I know how they voted and I'm furious with them ... how could they vote for Brexit? They weren't thinking about any generation apart from their own.' The same blanket contempt every time, no attempt to engage; merely hearing a different point of view is enough to drive them over the edge, so they close their ears and close their minds. Hope you enjoy Tbilisi, Pip.

The bizarre bullying. According to a TES Global poll of 750 teachers, at least 70 per cent voted for remain, and you would bet an even higher proportion in the south-east of our country. I spoke to one science teacher from London, Gareth Sturdy, who voted leave. He has now left the profession. 'It was the continual lambasting. The racists have taken over, the fascists are in charge. The hostility. But it was all group think. They weren't actually thinking about the issues at all.' He told me that a teaching colleague from another school had also left her job after it was revealed she had voted leave. 'An IT teacher pursued from the staff room, into the lab, into the library, haranguing her. She's now doing supply teaching.' And as Sturdy also commented, there was a direct threat to the careers of teachers who voted leave.

Group think indeed. In the previous chapter I tried to analyse the reasons for the leave vote, but in a sense the remain vote is a more interesting subject for investigation.

In 2012 the American sociologist Charles Murray wrote a book called *Coming Apart* in which he identified the rise of a new liberal elite that was almost perfectly cocooned from the rest of the country. I wrote about his book in the *Sunday Times*:

> It [the elite] is distanced geographically as well as cultur-ally: Murray notes that the 95th centile – the most well-off 5% of the population – increasingly live in gilded enclaves that he calls SuperZips. These are US postcodes where only the affluent live and there are growing clus-ters of them – in Washington, New York, San Francisco, Chicago – where that top 5% are truly insulated from the lives of the rest in their oases of affluence and civility. They mix only with people like themselves. They are increasingly liberated from the burden of having to turn up to such arcane concepts as an office. They have never done manual labour, they do not watch much TV. And they marry each other: whereas once we took as partners people we'd met in our home town, now we breed exclu-sively with people 'just like us', from within our adult milieu. Assortative mating or, as Murray puts it, homogamy.

The UK is not quite the same as the USA, but when you look at the remainer demographic you can begin to discern the same sort of thing happening here. The remain vote was at its strongest in Cambridge (but not, I would guess, Cherry Hinton), Oxford (but not Blackbird Leys), central London, parts of Bristol. But the geographical location,

while interesting, is of less import than the occupations of
the remainers in these areas. So, 96 per cent of the 'creative
community' voted remain. And 93 per cent of the academic
community. Add into that the aforementioned 70-odd per
cent of the teaching profession and 93 per cent of scientists.
And the media? What do you suppose the percentage is in
the BBC? I would hazard at about 99.9 per cent (see Chapter
6). I heard from one bloke who worked for the Corporation
and voted leave. He wouldn't give his name, rank or occu-
pation because he said he didn't want to lose his job. He
reckoned the only people working for the BBC who might
possibly have voted leave were the security staff.

And this is the thing. Leavers tend to know a lot of remainers. Probably a majority of my friends voted remain. But for
a hard core of the remain voters, when they say 'I don't know
anybody who voted leave', they mean it. They are not exag-
gerating. They literally never come into contact with the sort
of people who were stupid, racist or old enough to vote leave.
And they are closed minds, impervious to argument or
discussion. They are what John Gray describes as the 'hyper-
liberals', illiberal liberals, with special reference to universities: 'What happens on campus may not matter much in
itself. Anxiously clinging to the fringes of middle-class life,
many faculty members have only a passing acquaintance
with the larger society in which they live. Few have friends
who are not also graduates, fewer still any who are industrial
workers. Swathes of their fellow citizens are, to them, em-
bodiments of the Other – brutish aliens whom they seldom
or never meet. Hyper-liberalism serves this section of the
academy as a legitimating ideology, giving them an illusory

sense of having a leading role in society. The result is a richly entertaining mixture of bourgeois careerism with virtue-signalling self-righteousness – the stuff of a comic novel, though few so far have been up to the task of chronicling it.'

To be clear, this a minority of remain voters I am talking about. The majority of remainers will have done exactly as you or I did and weighed the issues and made their choice for rational reasons. Perhaps for reasons of self-interest, too, which is probably the most commendable and honest way to vote in any poll. Of my remainer friends, none want a second referendum. They were disappointed by the outcome of the vote and dismayed at the level of debate leading up to it, but nonetheless respect the outcome. That kind of view, I would guess, characterises the majority. And that hard core of remainers impervious to argument, aloof from discussion, perpetually furious? Perhaps about one-third of the remainer vote; the ones who defriend when they hear something with which they disagree. About four to five million or so people. In other words, Murray's ninety-fifth centile plus a few hundred thousand hangers on and wannabes (the teachers, then). And their insularity, protected by bubblewrap, explains some of the trauma that was occasioned to them and much of the rage.

Racist, thick, uneducated. So the mantra continued. The musician Billy Bragg asserted that while not all leave voters were racist, all racists voted leave. Howja know that, Bill? (I might add that while not all twats buy Billy Bragg records, everyone who buys a Billy Bragg record . . .)

But the racism thing became a theme, championed by the BBC and indeed much of the rest of the elite, as well as the remainer politicians and the academics. A university medical professor Mike Galsworthy, an outspoken remain campaigner, predicted that 'a rising tide of xenophobia' would discourage scientists from working in the UK. And yet the number of foreign academics working in the UK actually rose after the referendum result, as Cambridge University rather testily pointed out. Liberal Democrat leader Vince Cable characterised leave voters as people who possessed 'a nostalgia for a world where passports were blue, faces were white and the map of the world coloured imperial pink'. What, all of them, Vince? How about my twenty-one-year-old son? It is remarkably insulting, and politically stupid, to characterise the majority of the voting public in such a manner. The deplorable majority.

But the liberal media latched onto this xenophobia business, citing an 'enormous' rise in hate crimes, and especially racial hate crimes. The police did indeed report an, on the face of it, alarming 17 per cent rise in hate crimes year on year in April 2018, a report seized upon by the BBC and liberal media as evidence of the Brexit backlash against ethnic minorities and foreigners. What was not mentioned was the continual publicity given to the anti-hate crime agenda, its ubiquity in the media and the drive by the police to get people to report hate crimes, with posters in just about every pub lavatory. Nor did the reports mention the rather slender grounds upon which, these days, something can be reported as a hate crime. The leftish blog site Spiked Online did a bit of digging. Among the incidents categorised as 'hate crimes' were the following:

Dog shit found on the pavement outside a house.

A man accused of beeping his car horn 'in a racist manner'. The chap who beeped his horn had not been aware that the people he was beeping at were from a BME community.

A dog barking in a racist manner at someone.

A man who, while chatting to library staff, announced that he was campaigning to leave the European Union. The staff reported *that* as a hate crime.

A speech by the Conservative politician Amber Rudd on the subject of immigration. This was reported to the police as a 'hate crime' by an Oxford University professor who admitted he had not actually heard the speech, but had read about it later.

Nor did the news reports pay much attention to a study that came out in the same month and that showed that there had been a considerable lessening of animus towards migrants. 'UK attitudes towards immigration and free movement are noticeably more positive that before the referendum on June 23, 2016', the study concluded. Which institution produced this study? The European Union.

But it was crucial for the extremist remainer rump to keep plugging away at the inherent racism of the leave vote. It served to devalue the vote and to make opposition to a democratic process a point of principle.

If the xenophobia narrative persisted, so too did the notion that the leave voters were all thick as mince and hadn't known what they were doing. The People's Vote, a campaign for a second referendum, was launched in April 2018, based on the premise that those who had voted leave had not been aware of the complexities of the issues involved, the very real problems, the fine detail. Andy Parsons, the least funny comedian in the history of comedy, was there at the launch. So was the most staunch of the Labour remainers, Chuka Umunna. George Orwell would have appreciated Chuka's reasoning for a second vote: 'In our democracy, it is vital that the people get their say on Brexit, rather than their elected representatives in Parliament being reduced to some rubber stamp for whatever plan Boris Johnson, Jacob Rees-Mogg, and Michael Gove have been putting together behind closed doors.'

Of course, Parsons and Umunna and the rest of the People's Vote crowd had known all along how awful everything was going to be – they had voted remain. It was an act of kindness, then, to offer the dense lumpen *Untermensch* a chance to get it right at last. *They* didn't need another vote, only the thick northerners.

The People's Vote was also predicated on the assumption that many leave voters, bless them, had now changed their minds and wished for the country to remain within the EU. Plenty of opinion polls were suggesting the same thing and these were dutifully reported upon by, in particular, the BBC. And so, Sir John Curtice, Professor of Politics at the University of Strathclyde, appeared on the Radio 4 *Today* programme in late February 2019 with a model of polling figures that showed that there was a 'narrow but consistent' majority in recent polls for remaining in the EU, assuming (and it's a big assumption) that everybody turned out to vote. I don't doubt those figures (and still less Sir John's important caveats), but the polls have proven themselves to be very inaccurate of late. A six-point lead for remain may sound conclusive. But it is not as impressive as a ten-point lead for remain, which was reported in a Populus poll published on 22 June 2016. You take my point?

I'm sure some voters have changed their minds, in either direction. Perhaps more have changed their minds in favour of remaining, under the remorseless welter of propaganda and disinformation and opprobrium. But it might well be that as a consequence of this bullying leave voters are even less likely to tell the truth to pollsters about what way they would vote than they were on 22 June 2016. My suspicion, if there was another poll, is that if it were just a ratification of the 2016 vote and the leave side, in its campaign, insisted that it was simply a vote about respecting democracy, leave would win by a mile. But if there is another vote, it won't be that. It will be much as the People's Vote bores want it to be: between no deal, a bad deal and remain. In which case remain would of course win, the leave vote being split. Or a very bad deal versus remain.

There's certainly precedence for a second vote, as far as the EU is concerned. Every single time an EU member country has voted against some EU proposal, the opposition has either been effectively ignored (France and the Netherlands in 2005 on the plans for a EU Constitution, which quickly became the Lisbon Treaty) or forced to hold the referendum again and this time *get it right* (Ireland in 2001 on the Treaty of Nice and Denmark in 1992 on the Maastricht Treaty).

Whatever, the specious allegations of rampant xenophobia, the depiction of the leave voters as being changeable and not well informed all helped the remainer MPs – a huge majority – to assuage their possible guilt at ignoring the democratic mandate and slowly, over the course of two years, make their way to a position that wedded them to either a soft Brexit deal that was not Brexit at all, a plea for a second referendum or just to ignore the Brexit vote entirely. 'We must respect the wishes of the people' gradually became 'we must respect the will of the people, but . . .'

Not that gradually in many cases. Here's what that perpetually snippy Goliath among statesmen, John Major, had to say about the moral and political case for a second referendum, speaking before 23 June 2016: 'There will not be another referendum on Europe. This is it.' And here is what the former leader of the Liberal Democrats, the now late Paddy Ashdown, had to say before polling day: 'I will forgive no one who does not respect the sovereign voice of the British people once it has spoken. Whether it is a majority of 1 per cent or 20 per cent, when the British people have spoken, you do what they command. Either you believe in democracy or you don't.' And then there's this from Anna Soubry: 'We are trusting the British people. We will go to the people, and let the people decide whether or not to stay within the EU.'

All three later decided that actually we did need another vote. In Soubry's case, 24 June, just after lunch. She explained the apparent inconsistency by saying she had only made that ringing endorsement because she had expected remain to win. 'If I thought we'd lose, I wouldn't have said it, obviously.' Brilliant. And for this little slice of hypocrisy and deceit she was lauded as 'brave' by remainer commentators in the media.

The referendum gave MPs an order and a duty: get us out of the European Union. Not out of bits of it. Not to stay in. Not to have another vote. But all of the stuff I have outlined in this chapter helped them, in time, to renounce their commitments to the will of the people. From the Labour Party, which at first said it would respect the vote but is now demanding a Brexit so soft that it merely leaves us unrepresented chattels of the EU, to the Conservative remainers.

5

HERE COMES MAY

If David Cameron had been shocked by the result of the 2015 general election – and he certainly was – then it was nothing to the sense of bewilderment that settled upon him on the morning of 24 June a year later. Nobody had expected leave to win, least of all a Prime Minister who had proceeded with the referendum precisely because it was certain to result in a win for remain.

I suppose it is a tragedy for Cameron, a likeable man in private, that he will be remembered primarily for having brought chaos upon his party and the country, which is the view taken by many Conservative remainers. But then you might also argue that he had dug his own grave and then kept digging, deeper and deeper, before finally throwing himself into it. He had promised an in/out referendum in his famous Bloomberg speech of January 2013, when he also called for a reform of the European Union and at the least a recognition from Brussels that the UK would not always be moving in the same direction as its European partners – over a single currency and greater political alignment, for example. His aim here was to heal the splits within his own party over the EU – to stop MPs from 'banging on' about Europe, as he put it. That didn't quite work out, did it? At last, in February 2016, he was able to go to Brussels with a series of demands over closer political alignment, the single currency, benefits paid to immigrant workers, cutting bureaucracy and so on. He was listened to with varying degrees of politeness by the likes of Donald Tusk and given vague, evasively worded promises in a few areas and none whatsoever in others. His return to the UK was not in triumph, then, or certainly was not perceived as such.

You wonder how much the intransigence of the EU and Cameron's partial humiliation rested in the minds of voters as they made their way to the polls four months later. You wonder, too, if the EU might have been a little more *giving* had it taken seriously the prospect of a winning vote for leave that summer. But then Cameron did not expect a winning vote for leave. Truth be told, he had not expected the referendum to take place at all, when he committed himself to it in 2013: his pledge for one was made at a time when he was sure the Tories would lose the next election and the referendum idea would thus be the first thing to be jettisoned under an Ed Miliband-led Labour government, and even quicker if it was a coalition government with the Liberal Democrats. When we are studying the apparent political ineptitude that runs through this whole debacle like maggots in a chunk of rapidly decaying black pudding, so much of it is the consequence of perfectly clever politicians reading the polls – and the public – completely wrongly. And perhaps having too little faith in their own principles, if they have any.

Cameron looked at the result on 24 June and thought: *Fuck this. Why should I be lumbered with Brexit negotiations I never wanted or expected? I'm off.* And he resigned, on the spot, even as the tears were still flowing in the BBC studios and the pollsters were still gibbering their self-exculpatory idiocies. He resigned before his breakfast croissants had been served, at 06:27. But he would stay on, he explained, until his party had chosen a new leader and thus Prime Minister. As it happened, he didn't need to stay on for very long at all, because this was the first time in British history that May has followed June, following a series of events that, frankly, defy satire.

In February 2019, the Polish President of the European Council, Donald Tusk, said that 'a special place in Hell' would be found for the British Brexiteers who had demanded a vote for leave but failed to have even the most rudimentary idea of how to go about leaving. For this he was of course castigated by Brexiteers. But he had a point, surely. Because if Cameron was surprised by the win for leave, his shock was as nothing compared to that which visibly showed on the faces of the leaders of the leave campaigns (Nigel Farage excepted, although even he expected a defeat). They were utterly lost. No plan had been prepared for Brexit, nor for leadership succession (and they must have known that Cameron would resign if leave won).

Instead the Conservative leaders of the leave campaign staggered from microphone to microphone and tried very hard to look jubilant. For a country suddenly left in limbo there was no sense of direction, no notion of a strategy, no idea of how to proceed from here.

Their first recourse was to kick seven shades of shit out of each other for the prize of leading the Conservative Party, and thus becoming Prime Minister. Fair enough, I understand that imperative. But there was of course no unity among the leavers and no appetite for compromise. There were two obvious frontrunners for the premiership, Theresa May, the Home Secretary, who had backed remain, and Boris Johnson, easily the most recognisable and charismatic politician, Jeremy Corbyn and Nigel Farage aside, in the country. It may be that Boris actually won the vote for leave, having somewhat belatedly committed himself to the campaign.

Of these two candidates, Johnson was at first the clear favourite, both within the party and supposedly the public at large – an opinion poll earlier in the summer had placed him well ahead of Theresa May as the favourite to succeed David Cameron, possibly because he was the only Tory politician the vast majority of the public had heard of. But very quickly that lead was turned on its head: by the end of June, May was ahead by 31 per cent to Johnson's 24 per cent within the party, and May also had a lead within the public. The Home Secretary had a solid campaign team headed by the future (and not terribly successful) chief whip, Gavin Williamson. She also had money, via donations – far more than that available to Johnson. And there was a unity behind her. Johnson's most prominent supporter was the unquestionably talented Michael Gove, with whom Johnson had campaigned, week after week, for a leave vote. Three others announced their intention to run: the rightish Brexiteer Liam Fox, who probably didn't expect to win, the most pro-EU of them all, Stephen Crabb, and a woman called Andrea Leadsom, a leaver who was socially conservative and occupied the, uh, prestigious role of Minister of State for Energy. So, three leavers versus two remainers, one of whom (Crabb) stood no hope of winning. Already the leave side was deeply divided and found it impossible to coalesce around an agreed candidate.

It should be mentioned here that the Conservative Party is often perverse when it comes to leadership elections and rarely chooses the 'big beast' from the list of candidates. It did not do so when it elected as leader Margaret Thatcher, John Major, Iain Duncan Smith, William Hague or David Cameron. The only time in the last fifty years it went with the most renowned and experienced candidate was Michael Howard, in November 2003 (and look how that ended). So there is always hope for the outsider as a kind of compromise candidate: a compromise partly between what the party activists want and what the MPs in parliament want, but equally a bugger's muddle occasioned by the factional loathing within the parliamentary party. Anyway, we were headed towards a denouement that would surely result in a final run off between Theresa May and Boris Johnson, the other three candidates being eliminated along the way.

Until the following happened. Never underestimate the degree to which the great affairs of state are governed by vaulting ambition and magnificent, hitherto undisclosed, personal hatreds. Oh, and just pique.

On 30 June, just three hours before nominations closed, Boris Johnson's most prominent supporter, Michael Gove, announced his own candidacy. He had not, of course, advised Johnson's team that he would be doing so. He explained why he would be running in a statement put out to the press:

> Boris is a big character with great abilities and I enjoyed working with him in the referendum campaign, when he campaigned with great energy and enthusiasm.
>
> But there is something special about leading a party and leading a country, and I had the opportunity in the last few days to assess whether or not Boris could lead that team and build that unity.
>
> And I came reluctantly but firmly to the conclusion that while Boris has many talents and attributes, he wasn't capable of building that team. And there were a number of people who had said to me during the course of the week, 'Michael it should be you.'

I think my favourite bit of that statement is 'Michael, it should be you'. Gove took with him a sizeable chunk of Johnson's support within parliament, including the former chief whip Andrew Mitchell. Mitchell said: 'Michael Gove is the senior Brexiteer who put his country before his close friendship with David Cameron, and who has now reluctantly agreed to stand. Many Conservative MPs have, for years, suggested he was a highly credible candidate to be Prime Minister and now, with Brexit hanging over every aspect of British life, he is the man with the conviction, the courage and the capability to secure the best deal for Britain.'

I think it is fair to say that none of this went down terribly well with Boris Johnson, or his team. Gove was immediately accused of 'a systematic and calculated plot to destroy [Johnson]' and an act of 'midnight treachery', while Boris's dad, Stanley Johnson, muttered 'et tu, Brute'. The underworld was invoked, with one of Johnson's team insisting that there would be 'a very deep pit reserved in hell' for the supposedly treacherous Aberdonian. The allegation was that Gove had not, as he had informed the press, reluctantly and belatedly come to the conclusion that Boris was useless, but had been planning his little surprise for a considerable time – the circumstantial evidence for which lay in the speed with which half of Boris Johnson's supporters now cheerfully clambered aboard the Gove bandwagon. Johnson, shocked and infuriated, quickly did the math and came to the conclusion that he could not possibly win a leadership election: 'Having consulted colleagues and in view of the circumstances in Parliament, I have concluded that person cannot be me,' he said.

I haven't been able to find any senior Tories who *don't* think that Gove had this whole thing planned all along – apart from Gove. He maintains to this day that it was only in the week preceding the closing of nominations that he began to have grave doubts about his friend. In particular there was an incident when Andrea Leadsom turned up announcing that she would support Johnson, and not stand herself, if Boris made her either Chancellor of the Exchequer or Brexit Secretary – and she allegedly wanted a letter confirming this. To Gove's surprise – for he himself quite fancied one of those jobs – Johnson agreed immediately. 'This was the first element of things falling apart,' he said. Gove, one supposes, doubted the veracity of Johnson's promises regarding appointments and perhaps also felt that he could not rise to the occasion under the mantle of leadership. Gove might also cite his own rather dismal performance in the consequent leadership election as evidence that he had not been plotting at all: given more time he would surely have done a better job.

But there is also this. I know – or at least knew – Boris very well indeed. He was my editor at the *Spectator*. He is hugely good company, witty, loquacious and well read. He has undoubted charisma and usually a strong and imaginative grasp of the big picture, if not necessarily the fine detail. His success in being elected Mayor of London was quite remarkable, given the liberal-leftish mindset of the city – and he was not a bad mayor, either, as mayors go. Certainly better than the current incumbent. For these reasons, he is adored by the Conservative Party activists. Further, as Nigel Farage is only too happy to attest, Johnson's decision to join the leave campaign was, as Farage put it, decisive for their ability to win the day. The two politicians who should take most credit for the Brexit vote are Farage and Johnson.

But Boris is rather less well-loved by his parliamentary colleagues. Many, perhaps a majority, have grave reservations about him regarding his overweening ambition and the air of chaos that seems perpetually to follow him about. Senior Conservatives had been assuring me for years that Johnson could never win a leadership election. Perhaps Gove had done the maths, too, then.

Gove, Johnson, Osborne and Cameron. Four friends who had been in government together. Gove continued his friendship with Osborne despite backing leave. Johnson had by this time been estranged from the group. But of the four, Gove is the odd one out. He is the only one not possessed of a grand sense of entitlement to high office, a sort of divine right of kings, a consequence of their extremely expensive schooling and background. Gove was different, an adopted kid who attended a state school in Aberdeen. While the other three perhaps felt they would simply glide to high office, Gove never did. If he was to achieve it, perhaps it would take a little bit of midnight treachery.

Still, he got well and truly stuffed in the election. In the first ballot he polled just 14.6 per cent and came a poor third, way behind Theresa May on 50.2 per cent and even Andrea Leadsom on 20.1 per cent. Liam Fox was eliminated on 4.9 per cent and Stephen Crabb polled 10.3 per cent. Just to up the level of entertainment a little more, Crabb then withdrew from the contest when it was discovered he'd been sexting some nineteen-year-old lass (despite being married and forever banging on about family values, etc.). In the next round Gove's vote dropped down to 14 per cent and he was eliminated, with Leadsom on 25.5 and May on 60.5. That left a run off between May and Leadsom, but Leadsom then withdrew and a couple of weeks later re-emerged as the new Secretary of State for the Environment. Theresa May was Prime Minister, via a kind of belated coronation. Michael Gove would be out of office for the next twelve months.

Would Johnson's candidature have changed anything? My guess is that with Leadsom and Gove on board he might have been hovering around the 40 per cent mark – and thus would still have most likely lost in a final run off against Theresa May. Could anyone from the leave camp have beaten her? David Davis, for example? A poll in January 2016 suggested that two-thirds of Tory MPs were in favour of staying in the European Union, so the potential numbers may not have been there. But also, they are ever a divided, fissiparous, suspicious bunch, the leavers, as we have seen in the last two years: rarely able to agree among themselves and divided on other issues, too. But the fairly hilarious failure of the leave contingent to get their act in order, to subordinate their own doubts and loathings for the good of the cause, is one major reason why we are in the state we are in.

So, the country was now led by a Prime Minister determined to get the UK out of the EU but who had voted to keep us in it, while the Leader of the Opposition had supported the remain campaign but was a long-time advocate of leaving the EU (something many of his youthful followers in Momentum had failed to grasp). This defied satire. But being led by someone who had voted remain was crucial in the negotiations that would follow with the EU. They knew, from the start, that her heart was not in it. They knew she would be rather more open to compromise than, say, Johnson or Gove. It queered the pitch before the game had even started.

6

IN SPITE OF BREXIT

The BBC behaved itself in the run up to the June 2016 referendum. It had to. It was required to do so by law, under the Representation of People Act. And so it acted in an even-handed manner toward the two competing sides – to the extent that some in the remain lobby were furious at its palpable lack of bias. They complained long and loud that in giving equal airtime to each side, the BBC was ignoring the crucial fact that they were right and the leavers were wrong. An excellent example of this approach was reported by the *Sunday Times*'s political editor Tim Shipman, who quoted an un-named and unhappy member of the Britain Stronger in Europe board: 'They [the BBC] got obsessed about having to have equal billing on every side of the argument. You'd have the IMF, then you'd have a crackpot economist, or you'd have a FTSE 100 CEO and then someone who makes a couple of prams in Sheffield. It was balanced in terms of the amount of coverage, but not balanced in terms of the *quality* [my italics] of people.'

Well, indeed: the egregious *quality* of these leavers. But not to worry. As soon as the result was in, the gloves came off: the tenor changed a little. And what followed was two and a half years of relentlessly, odiously biased coverage in BBC news and current affairs and well beyond – spreading happily into the comedy, light entertainment and drama output. The title of this chapter is a standing joke among Brexiteers: every bit of good economic news reported by the BBC would begin with the words 'in spite of Brexit . . .' Propitious economic news was invariably played down or heavily caveated and the headlines taken up with outrageous predictions of imminent catastrophe. The BBC also focused upon highly dubious stories of Brexit endangering the lives of immigrants to the country, and continued its relentlessly pro-immigration line whenever the subject arose. Its bias has been patent and relentless. It happened night after night, for thirty months.

The Corporation now had a new trick up its sleeve: a 'reality checker' by the name of Chris Morris. His job was to pop up and tell viewers who, of the debating politicians, had their facts right. But of course he is no less imbued with the same bias as his employers: Mr Morris spouted the BBC's pro-remainer line almost every time he opened his mouth. The former Conservative minister Peter Lilley, now Lord Lilley, crossed swords with Morris after Morris had been wheeled out to refute everything Lilley had said about negotiating a free trade deal. It was clear, from their heated exchange, that these were simply two sides of an argument and that Mr Morris was no more rooted in reality than was Peter Lilley. As Lord Lilley said shortly afterwards: 'He [Morris] systematically argued the Remain case and defended their Project Fear scare stories. The one thing he did not do was bring in any new facts. My central claim was that if we leave the EU Customs Union but have a free trade agreement with the European Union, our businesses have little to fear.'

Morris had previously been responsible for a five-part radio series, *Brexit: A Guide for the Perplexed*. Mr Reality Checker used twenty-four main interviews for this unbiased, unpartisan delectation – of which eighteen were speaking from an anti-Brexit perspective. Only 7 per cent of the words throughout the course of this series were spoken by people who were in favour of doing what the country had voted to do – leave the European Union. I heard this series. It could not have been more biased if it had been presented by Lord Mandelson.

Morris and the Reality Check team are used by the BBC to deliver a verdict on everything – and it is my contention that they do so from an invariably partisan, liberal position, in common with almost all of the BBC's output. In the case of Brexit, I think that assertion is very clearly proven. But even if they were not institutionally biased, the 'reality check' operation is a patently absurd and insultingly simplistic confection. As I'm writing this, the BBC Reality Check team – a mere handful of people – are pronouncing the sole truth on the following disputatious issues: Donald Trump's speech regarding wage growth in the USA (Trump's lying, natch); have the Oscars fixed their diversity problem?

(Nope); what does a World Trade Organization no deal exit mean for Britain? (Plague, killer bees, death); rent control – does it work? (Sometimes, up to a point); and does dry January lead to binge February? (Sorry, I'd lost the will to live by this point and read no further.) And that's just today. Just one day in the lives of the tiny Reality Check team. It must be hugely comforting, if you are a credulous idiot, to know that despite all the enormous contention in this teeming, complex, fissiparous world of ours, there are five people sitting in New Broadcasting House who are the sole repositories of the truth about absolutely everything, less mere oracles than actual gods. The only pristine guardians of what is correct.

Quite how this makes the likes of Laura Kuenssberg or Jon Sopel, both eminent BBC correspondents, feel is beyond me. Are they not speaking the truth, when they report from Westminster or Washington? Should they not be subject, after each two-way with Huw or John, to an analysis by the Reality Checkers, so that we can know for sure they're not lying?

I suspect the reality-check stuff was brought in following those remainer gripes during the referendum campaign, and also as a kind of backstop, if you'll excuse the term, against that awful thing, fake news. But 'fake news' is very often simply news that some people of a certain political disposition – right or left – merely wish was untrue. The uncomfortable truth is that there is no single discernible truth – and certainly not when we're dealing with predictions for the future made by institutions with skin in the game.

Basically, the busy little Reality Check team read a couple of reports on each issue and pick out the things they think are important and are then empowered by the BBC to tell the world that this is *fact*. Here's a reality check for you, Chris Morris and Lord Hall: that's what we all do, you know? Leavers and remainers. Think tanks and governments. Journos and normal people. We read a few things and make up our minds. The only difference is that the rest of us still have doubt, except for the nutters.

The biased output of the BBC in the first few months following the referendum got so bad that, in March 2017, a total of seventy-two MPs from all parties wrote an open letter complaining about the 'pessimistic and skewed' coverage of the Brexit issue. As Robin Aitken put it, in his 2018 book about the BBC's institutional bias, *The Noble Liar*, the MPs were not simply angry at the mood of 'neurotic pessimism' – which was already in evidence in the BBC studio at 04:40 on 24 June when David Dimbleby announced that leave had won, that gnashing of teeth and wailing and expressions of contempt and loathing directed towards the majority – but those aforementioned caveats: 'in spite of Brexit' followed by a spurious reality check that we were all headed to hell in a handcart. In spite of Brexit, employment is up, unemployment is down, inward investment is up, wages are rising, inflation is steady, consumer spending is up . . . all despite Brexit. That the BBC's previous predictions, based upon flawed reports from the likes of the Bank of England and the International Monetary Fund, had been proven wrong was beyond doubt. But hell, here was a BBC reality checker to assure you that they would be proven right, in a bit, eventually, one day. Quoting the same institutions who had made those fatuous predictions before, and doing so without a vestige of irony or self-awareness. The BBC took not the slightest notice of that open letter. Its response was, effectively, fuck you.

Kamal Ahmed was the BBC's Economic s Editor and is now Director of Editorial News at the corporation. (There are more middle management positions in the BBC than you could possibly dream of. I haven't got a clue what a Director of Editorial News does. When I worked there my line manager for a while was Managing Editor News and Current Affairs Programmes, i.e. MENCAP, an acronym that I always reckoned had a certain ring of truth about it.) Kamal, ex-*Guardian* and *Observer*, natch, is a bright and affable bloke. He also resembles, physically, a pencil that has been sharpened to slightly beyond its optimum length. None of this really matters, of course. What matters is the email he sent to all BBC journalists, and uncovered by the Guido Fawkes website, reminding them that whatever Brexiteers might think or say, the economists are right – Brexit is 'a bit rubbish'. His economists, you will note: not all economists, by a long shot. The economists of whom he took notice. The very ones who had made the flawed predictions about what would happen immediately if the UK voted to leave the European Union. The BBC's official line, then, dutifully handed down to the staff – as if they needed such corporate nudging.

Having ignored the MPs when they complained, the BBC didn't take much greater interest in a report compiled by the Institute for Economic Affairs (IEA), which suggested that on both the programmes *Question Time* and *Any Questions*, Brexit voices were seriously and serially under-represented, post referendum. You may have noticed, listening to or watching these programmes, that there is never a pro-Brexit majority on the panel. I cannot remember such a thing on *Question Time* in more than two years – the odds are always four to one in favour of remain or three to two at best. It's a point I've sometimes thought of making when I'm on one of those shows, but it seems, at the time, petty and ill-mannered. I should have more of a spine and less of a worry about the BBC's sensibilities. The IEA added up all the appearances: 68 per cent in favour of remain, 32 per cent in favour of Brexit. The think tank concluded:

> The imbalance on the two programmes is substantial, consistent and at odds with public opinion. The analysis reveals a two to one bias in favour of those who voted for remain.
>
> Brexit is probably the most defining issue of the UK policy debate at present and as such should be vital in balance. For the vast majority of both programmes, Brexit has been the most dominant issue discussed on both programmes. Both shows appear to accept the predominance of Brexit as an issue, but by the selection of panellists seem to attach a low priority to balancing the panel on the topic.

OK, so *Question Time*, in particular, has a lot of very onerous balancing to do, granted. It needs to give proportionate coverage to the various parliamentary parties – and

parliament has an inbuilt remainer majority. It also feels
the compulsion to strike a gender balance and make sure
there is always one black or minority ethnic person on each
week, although why it should be quite so rigorous in this
last matter eludes me, given that our BME community is
not yet anywhere near 20 per cent of the national population. But still, it feels enjoined to respect those guidelines
– but not the fact that a majority of the public was in favour
of leave. On the biggest issue in British politics for seventy
years, the story that has dominated the news for the past
two and a half years, the BBC's most important political
programme has been hideously biased against one side.

The BBC has form on this issue. When I was editor of
BBC Radio 4's flagship morning news programme *Today*,
back at the turn of the present century, I received a letter
from a gentleman called Baron Pearson of Rannoch,
politely requesting a meeting to discuss my programme's
coverage of European issues. At the time, the biting issue
was principally about whether or not we should join the
European single currency, but there was also a tranche of
Conservative MPs who wished us to leave the EU altogether
as well as the Referendum Party, set up by the financier Sir
James Goldsmith (and of which Lord Pearson was a
member), which campaigned for a vote on leaving the EU.

I met Malcolm Pearson for a coffee and he unloaded his
grievances. He had done a long study of the BBC's output,
he told me, and added up the minutes afforded to pro- and
anti-European Union speakers. It showed an enormous
bias in favour of those who were pro-EU. I told Malcolm
that I accepted entirely the generality of his complaint and

would do something about it. But I was less impressed by his methodology, this adding up of the minutes. At the time the country was ruled by a very pro-European Labour Party, which basked in a huge majority. The Conservative Party in parliament was at least 60 per cent pro-EU and the Liberal Democrats (then sizeable in their parliamentary representation) and the nationalist parties entirely pro-EU. How, given that balance of power in Westminster, could I be expected to give equal time to fewer than half of the beleaguered official opposition and a fringe party that had no representation at all? But I agreed with him on the generality of his complaint. It seemed to me (as a Labour Party member at the time) that the BBC was indeed heavily biased against those who were in favour of leaving the EU and those who objected to the idea of a single European currency.

I reported my discussion to a very senior BBC manager, the controller of editorial policy, and added that I thought Baron Pearson of Rannoch had a strong case. 'You have to understand, Rod,' she said to me, 'that these people are mad.' Ah, indeed. In fairness to the woman, this was precisely the view of almost everybody else at the BBC. Eurosceptics were all xenophobic dinosaurs and their views absurd. All I had to do to get a laugh at *Today*'s morning meeting was mention the name 'Bill Cash' and the giggling would start.

Anyway, I kept a closer eye on the pro- and anti-EU balance on the programme and commissioned a series of investigations into the EU's 'secret' proposals for greater political alignment and even a European defence force.

These reports were castigated by Tony Blair's chief of staff, Alastair Campbell, as being entirely untrue: the EU intended no such thing. As so often seemed to be the case, Alastair was lying. I hope Malcolm Pearson enjoyed those reports. But he wasn't finished counting up those minutes of airtime. The BBC was eventually forced to commission an independent inquiry into Malcolm's complaints in the autumn of 2004. The Wilson Report, published the following January, largely vindicated Pearson and concluded: 'although the BBC wishes to be impartial in its news coverage of the EU, it is not succeeding'. But the imbalance continued, quite unabated. Pearson later became an early leader of UKIP.

I have reconsidered my objections to Pearson's methodology. I still find the totting up of airtime minutes a little coarse and reductionist, but then what else was he to do? It was the only way to prove, objectively, substantively, that the BBC was showing a grotesque bias. Everything else could be written off as subjective: the tone of a presenter's questioning, the harder ride given to Eurosceptic interviewees, the story selection, the occasional slipped asides – all subjective and anecdotal. Which is why the Wilson Report and the report I mentioned previously from the Institute for Economic Affairs are important. They both prove the case. And they have both been effectively ignored.

I don't know how you actually 'prove' the rest of the stuff. The comedy panel shows that are perpetually anti-leave (and also anti-Trump). The documentaries skewed in favour of remain. The propaganda making its way even into such programmes as *Doctor Who* where, in one episode, watched by an ever-dwindling audience by now bored into a catatonic stupor by the programme's right-on virtue signalling, an alien invasion of Earth (or something) could not be thwarted because our planet had recently left an intergalactic federation and was now alone. Get it, you mugs? Viewers rang in to complain: the BBC told them to get stuffed. The commissioning of programmes by Radio 4 always by pro-EU presenters, such as the undoubtedly talented David Aaronovitch.

The Wilson Report made it clear that the BBC did not think it *was* being biased, even though it unquestionably was biased. The bias, then, was unconscious. I think that's a reasonable explanation – and it is one reason why I have some sympathy for left wingers who believe the BBC is biased against them. It is not a left-wing bias that infects the BBC – the Corporation gives Jeremy Corbyn and John McDonnell a very hard time. It's a liberal bias, which they do not think is political at all: it's just an expression of civility and decency. They swallow all the intersectional rubbish, they approve of immigration because it's being 'nice', they dislike Euroscepticism because it smacks of xenophobia and they do not think that any of this is remotely political, because they all think exactly the same way.

I know an awful lot of people in the BBC. I do not know a single one who voted leave. I was told by a chap at *Newsnight* that at the very most one person out of the entire staff had voted leave. I was mildly surprised it was that many. I am Facebook friends with lots of BBC people: all of them remainers, every single one. The Corporation has become a vast echo chamber of polite middle-class opinion, utterly bereft of political diversity. And so, when the Wilson Report comes out, or the study from the IEA, they are astonished that their mindset should be criticised, because almost everyone within the Corporation thinks the same thing. And those who don't think the same thing are mad or beyond the pale. And yet this consensus is not remotely shared by the population that pays for the BBC and that thinks that perhaps there are downsides to uncontrolled immigration and that the nation state might be a better bet than a European superstate and is tired of the BBC's bizarre obsessions with race and gender politics.

In March 2019 the magazine *Prospect* ran, as its cover story, a long essay about the dangers posed to the BBC by the Brexit debate. Confidence in the Corporation's impartiality was rapidly diminishing, apparently – well, yes, goodness me, whodathunk it, etc. The article was by a man called Mark Damazer, of whom you may not have heard. Mr Damazer was formerly a middle manager at the BBC: Assistant Director of BBC News for a while and also Controller of Radio 4. His background? Go on, take a wild guess. North London suburbs, public school, Oxbridge – and he's now running some Oxbridge college, which is what almost all BBC panjandrums end up doing once the Beeb has spat them out like a kind of gilded, privileged owl pellet. Mr Damazer was one of my plethora of bosses when I was running the *Today* programme and I found him – like I found many of them – charming, erudite, civilised and kindly of manner, as well as being so magnificently divorced from the realities that afflicted the majority of his listeners that he might as well have hailed from a distant planet perhaps somewhere in the disputed Tadpole Galaxy, 420 million light years from Earth.

I have one abiding memory of Mark's management, from around about the turn of the present century. An American election was in the offing and the editors of the news and current affairs programmes were all summoned to his office to be told that our coverage must not under any circumstances be biased, no matter how much we despised George W. Bush. It must be fair. It must give adequate weight to either side. Mark was sitting at his desk in his grand office; we were sat facing him. And as this excellent homily was delivered occasionally our eyes would wander to the large wall behind Mark's head, and the myriad of posters on it, all from US election campaigns in which Mark had actively taken part. 'Vote Democrat!' they all read – every single one. 'Vote Simon – Democrat!' Loads of lovely old posters, every single one urging victory for the Democrats. Nobody mentioned it and I don't think Mark saw the irony.

No surprise, then, that in his long essay for *Prospect* magazine Mark seemed appalled that one side was not being treated fairly. Which side? The remain side. Not enough fact checking to challenge these dimbo leaver bastards was the basic gist. A long, nay interminable, peroration. No mention of the basic problem that there are simply no leavers working for the BBC: they do not exist. No notion that this extraordinary lack of representation might queer the pitch a little on such an important debate. No mention, anywhere in his piece, of the House of Commons petition about the relentless pro-remain bias of the BBC. No mention of the IEA study that proved, utterly, the pro-remain bias on *Question Time* and *Any Questions*. (There are facts for you, Damazer, if you'd care to look.) Nope, for Marky Mark the chief problem was journalism of insufficient rigour to unsettle the leaver cause. Poor bloke. He has glided from the echo chamber of Oxbridge to the echo chamber of the BBC and now with consummate grace back, back, in the other direction whence he came. A life of exquisite white middle-class privilege, which has not only blinded him to how the output of his old Corporation sounds to those who do not remotely share his half-baked, intellectually bereft, liberal views, and which he does not really think are views at all. But which also somehow insulates him from empirical evidence. And yet Damazer – a nice man, as I've mentioned – is not alone in this. He is instead completely typical within the BBC.

Every year the BBC broadcasts something called The Reith Lectures, in which someone very bloody self-important puts us right about stuff. In 2019 it was the fabulously pompous judge Jonathan (Lord) Sumption (Eton and Oxford, natch), telling us how he appalled he was by the 'totalitarian' attitudes of leave voters: because the vote in the referendum was close, the decision of the people should not be respected as such, but subject to negotiation and conciliation. This is a very bitter and shallow reading, to my mind. You can either leave the EU, as the referendum insisted, or not leave it. A half way house is effectively not leaving it. On some issues there is no middle way, sadly. If the referendum had been about capital punishment and the pro-hangers had won by a narrow margin, what would Sumption have said then? Where is the middle way? But my real point here is that the BBC once again decided to give uncontested airtime to an enemy of Brexit. Can you imagine the Reith Lectures being delivered by someone in favour of withdrawal, or in favour of halting immigration, or banning gay marriages? It simply wouldn't happen.

Back in November 2018 I was driving in my car and put on the *PM* programme. One of the lead stories was about the American mid-term primaries and the show carried a very long report from Jim Naughtie, who had been out there covering the elections. It was a superb piece of journalism, beautifully written, nuanced, even-handed and with revelatory interviews with ordinary US voters. I know Jim from way back. He is a liberal remainer; we share very few of the same views. But he is an excellent journalist and he is at his best out on the hoof, talking to people. And I mention this only to highlight how sad I feel about sticking the boot into the BBC, given that once in a while it will throw up something as good as Jim's report from the US. But the problem seems to me insuperable. Confined in its bubble, the Corporation has lost the country; lost even the ability to empathise with the country beyond the M25. And it can't see it, no matter how many reports are commissioned that point out the unpalatable truth.

A week before I wrote this chapter, the BBC had been at it again. It had reported on its news programmes, prominently, that people would not be able to book tickets on Brittany Ferries after 26 March 2019 because of Brexit. Brittany Ferries reacted with apoplexy and immediately tweeted that the BBC would have 'worried many customers' with a report that was 'nonsense'. Not only could people of course still book their tickets, but Brittany Ferries had expanded its fleet so there were even more tickets to go around. The BBC has been perhaps the most valuable weapon in the remainer armoury. That it doesn't think it is a weapon at all makes the tragedy even greater.

7

LONDON

London was the only region in England to vote remain and did so by a hefty margin – 59.9 to 40.1 per cent. Just five boroughs voted to leave, and they were far flung, on the outer margins of the capital, in what we used to call the 'white flight' suburbs. So Havering, then – right at the end of the District line, basically Romford, Upminster and Hornchurch, the places the old Eastenders were shipped out to after their communities had been bombed flat in the war, now set up in rapidly and cheaply built social housing estates nudging the boundaries of Essex. Havering was 70 per cent for leave and its next-door neighbour, Barking and Dagenham, with a similar if slightly less affluent demographic, 62 per cent. Then way out west to Hillingdon (Heathrow, Uxbridge, middle-class Ruislip), down to the extreme south-east in my old borough, Bexley, and just a dozen or so miles to the west, Sutton, with one foot hovering over Surrey. Those were the boroughs that voted to leave. In a couple of others, such as Hounslow, also on the edge of London, the result was very close. But overall, London was very strongly for remain and, by and large, the closer you get into the centre, the greater the margin of victory. Why?

The distance between London and the rest of the country increases seemingly by the week. For many of those who live beyond the M25 the capital is a city state where things are done differently; foreign, aloof, disdainful of the provinces and possessed of beliefs that are often antithetical to those of 'middle England' (the slightly contemptuous term applied to the entire country, London excepted). The referendum result was an expression of this distance, although it is also true to say the remain vote also tended to do well in the metropolitan centres of our biggest provincial cities, from Bristol to Newcastle. But there is something different about London; the weight it has, its affluence, its attractiveness (the most popular city with tourists in Europe). You can take two views of London, or maybe haver somewhere in between. As Londoners see it, the capital is an exemplar of liberal multiculturalism, an extraordinarily diverse mix of peoples working together in a kind of harmony, for the benefit of all. This is how a city should be, they think, tolerant and diverse, not insular and monocultural. And then there is the other view, that London's affluence is in part the direct consequence of its exploitation of a vast and largely foreign service class, characterised by low skills, low wages and often shocking, overcrowded accommodation. I tend to subscribe to something close to the latter view. My suspicion is that for the affluent white Londoners it is a case of economic self-interest masquerading as tolerant inter-nationalism. But still, the exploited and the exploiters were able to happily come together to vote remain.

The remain vote was its highest in those London boroughs with the highest proportion of immigrants, or the children of immigrants. In Haringey, only 34.7 per cent of residents are classified as white British and the borough voted 75 per cent remain. A similar story in Lambeth, where only 39 per cent of people are white British and 78 per cent voted remain. The remain vote was the same in Hackney, where only 36 per cent of people are white British. White British people are now a minority in the majority of London boroughs. There are fairly obvious reasons why immigrants, or the children of immigrants, might take exception to Brexit. First, they are inclined to see inward immigration in a kinder light, having been immigrants or the children of immigrants themselves. A Runnymede Trust report from 2017 also suggested that black and minority ethnic Britons felt that the Brexit debate might impact negatively upon them, a consequence of the focus upon immigration and that also they felt more 'positively' about immigration than the average British voter (despite also wishing to see it limited). There is no great surprise in any of that. But then there is also this: if you are a fairly recent arrival in this country, does its long existence as a nation state matter very much to you? Do you have a stake in our history? Is the UK's history as an independent country as impinging as it might be on someone whose family has lived here for countless generations? It may well be too that as an immigrant from beyond Europe, from one of our former colonies, your view of Britain's status as a nation state, and its history, may have a certain taint to it, and for good reason. So on both of the leading issues promulgated by the Brexiteers – sovereignty and immigration – the vast bulk of London's ethnic minority population, and thus about half of its total population, was inherently averse or simply uninterested. They voted overwhelmingly for remain.

The influx of immigrants into London boroughs has been vast, rapid and very recent. To take Haringey as an example, the white British contingent comprise 34.7 per cent of the borough today, while in 2001 that figure was almost 60 per cent. That is an enormous transformation in a very short period of time indeed, and broadly the same sort of changes have taken place in Hackney, Tower Hamlets, Southwark, Lewisham and Newham. I wonder which side would have won in London if the referendum had been held in 2001? You would bet on the figures being much, much closer.

But by and large the white British in London voted the same way – or, at least, they did if they were affluent and not living in the white flight outer circle. It may well be that these people consider the European Union to be a singularly noble institution and like to think of themselves as primarily European, rather than British, sharing a common culture with the French and the Italians, a love of food, wine and agreeable holidays. It may be too that they approve of the Polish builders excavating their basements for half the going rate, much as they approve of their cheap au pairs from Slovakia, Uber taxi drivers from Afghanistan, and so on. Economic self-interest, again, surely plays a part, even if it is rarely acknowledged. But there is nothing wrong with economic self-interest when it comes to voting. The point is that, perhaps uniquely, the Brexit referendum was won for remain in London by a convocation of very well-off white people and black and brown people who were not very well off at all. A remarkable alliance.

Post referendum, London became crucial to the remain cause, as an entity, as the focus for remainer dissent and as a centre for channelling money into multifarious campaigns to thwart Brexit, delay Brexit, postpone Brexit, re-run Brexit and so on. On New Year's Eve 2018, the pro-remainer Mayor of London, Sadiq Khan, had commissioned a firework display which many leave voters considered a multimillion-pound festival of trolling. The London Eye was lit up with the colours of the European Union flag and as the fireworks were detonated along the Thames, the words 'London Is Open' were broadcast in English, French, German, Spanish, Italian and Romanian. I don't know what the poor old Poles had done to get left out. Perhaps Khan does not like their Eurosceptic government much more than he likes the right-ish government in Hungary. The message, anyway, was intended to distance London from the rest of the UK and for Europeans to understand that whatever those insular clowns did in the rest of the country, London – an important bit of the country, perhaps the only important bit – was still four-square behind the EU. But then, London's politicians had been unequivocal ever since the referendum that this whole Brexit business should simply be ignored.

Take, for example, the Labour MP for Tottenham, David Lammy. It took David a full hour from hearing the referendum result to demanding that it must be ignored completely. Fuck democracy – just ignore it. 'Wake up,' he insisted. 'We do not have to do this. We can stop this madness and bring this nightmare to an end through a vote in Parliament. Our sovereign Parliament needs to now vote on whether we should exit the EU.' The result, he insisted, was 'not binding' – a familiar refrain from the dog days of summer 2016 on the part of remainers who seemed to cleave to the view that votes were only 'binding' if they went the right way.

In a leafier part of London, a British-Guyanese businesswoman called Gina Miller, née Singh, was sitting down to a traumatised breakfast with her children. She had slept for only thirty-six minutes, apparently, the night before, so aghast was she at the result. One of her children said to her: 'But you'll do something, Mummy – you always do,' according to Miller herself. I'd have liked the kid more if he'd said: 'Never mind, Mummy. It's the will of the people, democratically expressed. Now pass the fucking cornflakes.' But she did indeed do something and we are enjoined to admire her 'guts' and 'resolve' for doing so, rather than considering her an undemocratic narcissist. She engaged very expensive lawyers to take the government to court over the issue of Article 50 of the Treaty on the European Union, insisting that it could not be invoked using prerogative powers without the will of parliament.

She was doing this, she insisted – and this is what the remainer extremists always insist, no matter how absurd it might sound – in the name of democracy. In other words, a decision made by the British people was now dependent upon a bunch of unelected and liberally minded judges who, to nobody's great surprise, concurred with Ms Miller.

I have no doubts about the clear independence of the judiciary from both our government and general political interference – but then nor do I believe that the views of their lordships are entirely independent from the mindset of the ruling elite: they are, after all, part of it. I didn't believe it during the Jeremy Thorpe trial in 1979 and I don't believe it now. The judiciary is ever a captive of the ruling culture, whatever that culture might be. In the end, Miller's expensive intervention probably strengthened Theresa May's hand because, after an appeal, the government went straight ahead and called a parliamentary vote on the invocation of Article 50, which it won with ease. Oh dear, Mummy. However, Miller's intervention was crucial in passing the decision-making process into the hands of the politicians (who were in favour of remain) and away from the people who had voted.

But this trope, this notion, is that everything is more democratic than the vote we had. Everything we, the remainers, suggest serves to extend that expression of suffrage, to make it even more democratic. Here are a few of the things that, at various times, remain supporters have suggested would be even more democratic than respecting the democratic vote taken by the British people on 23 June 2016:

- getting Parliament to vote on whether we should leave or not (i.e. ignoring the referendum);
- allowing the judiciary to decide whether we can simply leave or not (i.e. ignoring the referendum);
- allowing the House of Lords to decide whether we can leave or not (i.e. ignoring the referendum);
- simply not leaving (ignoring the referendum entirely);
- revoking Article 50 because it is disastrous and somehow, therefore, undemocratic (i.e. ignoring the referendum);
- having another vote (yes, yes, ignoring the referendum).

All of these, at one time or another, have been described as a more democratic alternative to abiding by the vote of the referendum.

Gina Miller and David Lammy were the first Londoners to mobilise. The rest soon followed, a plethora of organisations dedicated to fighting Brexit, all situated in London and funded through donations from rich businessmen, such as George Soros or the boss of Superdry, Julian Dunkerton – that is, when they weren't funded directly by the European Union through your taxes. Oh, and also by third sector charities, some of which receive funding direct from the state.

So, for example, Labour for a People's Vote, situated in Millbank Tower, London SW1, receives donations from the Joseph Rowntree Foundation and, bizarrely, the anti-racist organisation Hope Not Hate (presumably on the grounds that anyone who voted leave must be a racist, a familiar theme from remainers and explicitly stated by London MP Diane Abbott, as I have mentioned). Meanwhile, Healthier in the EU and Scientists for EU were set up by Mike Galsworthy, from the London School of Hygiene and Tropical Medicine. Both organisations come under the umbrella of the People's Vote and have their offices in Millbank Tower, along with InFacts, Open Britain (which campaigned against the reselection of MPs who supported leave), For Our Future's Sake (students against Brexit), Our Future Our Choice (nice young people who aren't students against Brexit) and Britain for Europe.

The European Movement sits right alongside these lot in Millbank Tower. A cross-party coalition determined to fight Brexit, it recently received funding of 350,000 euros direct from the EU: in other words, leave voters contributed their own cash, unwillingly. The extremely pro-federalist European Alternatives has its British headquarters a short distance outside the capital, in Letchworth Garden City, Hertfordshire. Hell, at least they probably bump into people who voted leave from time to time. European Alternatives was recently bunged 300,000 euros from the EU (i.e. your taxes, again) to continue its important and exciting work pressing for a vast, socialistic, European superstate.

The People's Vote hold marches, and when they march, they march in London. And the marchers are addressed by that familiar retinue of London celebs: the inevitable Gary Lineker, impressionist Rory Bremner, the unbiased broadcaster Gavin Esler and the side-splittingly funny comedian Andy Parsons.

The merchant banks, the big businesses and the metropolitan 'artistic community' (luvvies, etc.) add their voice
to this fugue of whining and complaint. The powerful in
our capital city do not like being gainsaid, nor are they
accustomed to being so.

8

THE CALLING OF THE
2017 ELECTION

A Downing Street spokesperson told a briefing of journalists in Westminster on Monday morning: 'There is no change in our position on an early general election. <u>There is not going to be a general election</u>.

Independent, 20 March 2017

In the mid-morning of 18 April 2017, the Westminster press corps was informed by Downing Street that the Prime Minister would be making an important statement in a short while. The hacks didn't have a clue what was going on, so all they could do was speculate, on air and off. Most assumed Theresa May was ill – maybe something to do with her diabetes – and that she might be stepping down, either temporarily or permanently. They certainly didn't think she was going to call a general election because she had told them repeatedly that she would not consider such a thing.

And so, just before lunchtime, Theresa May announced to the country that there would be a general election on 8 June. She stood just outside the front door to 10 Downing Street, wearing a smart grey suit that betokened serious-ness and grave import. She spoke with the earnest and implacable confidence of a village idiot and mentioned the word 'stability' several times. There is a string on Theresa May's back, hidden from the cameras. If you pull it, she'll say 'stability', over and over again, and sometimes 'certainty'. Someone had given it a good tug that lunchtime.

This announcement of a snap election took everyone, not just the Westminster journos, by surprise for a couple of reasons. First, we are now supposed to have fixed-term parliaments (with the next one therefore due in 2020) and, second, as I mentioned, she had spent the last six months assuring anyone who enquired that there was not the remotest prospect of her calling an election because it would not be in the country's interests to do so. What the country needed at this moment in time, she would go on to say, as the cameras rolled, was stability and certainty – and you don't get that sort of thing by calling an election. Her office last denied there would be a snap general election less than one month before she actually called one, as you can see from the quote above.

Why did she call it, then? Simple answer: to provide the country with more stability and certainty, she explained. She had just chaired a meeting of the cabinet and they were all agreed, she kind of implied just outside No. 10: we must have an election. This decision was presented to the public as a case of the Prime Minister, representing Brexit, versus parliament, representing remain. The Augean stables needed clearing out, to give her a clearer majority and therefore a stronger mandate to continue negotiations with the EU. This was to be a Brexit election, then. Except that it wasn't. Brexit was the dog that didn't bark throughout the entire, lamentable campaign. But it was also her attempt to de-Cameronise the government, to stamp her own authority on her party, her own image, an image that stood for stability and certainty, apparently.

As it happened, there were quite a few Conservative politicians, including some cabinet members, who were not at all convinced by the need for an election. Despite the opinion polls, not all of them thought it a mere formality that she would increase her majority. The voting public can be a volatile beast; it can be wayward and unpredictable. Bizarrely, you might think, it has a mind of its own.

Still, looked at superficially, you can see why a snap election held promise for May. Her working majority that lunchtime in mid-April was only seventeen; Lord, how she would be happy with that now. More to the point, Labour was floundering and seemed beyond redemption. The three opinion polls carried out on 17 and 18 April put Jeremy Corbyn's party a minimum of 18 points behind in the polls (and a maximum of 21) and Jeremy Corbyn's personal ratings were 30 points below those of Theresa May's. You looked at Corbyn's hopelessly divided Labour Party, marooned in the mid-20s in the polls and led by a chap who seemed an unappealing hybrid of Catweazle, Chauncey Gardner and Vladimir Lenin, and thought: call an election – what can possibly go wrong?

Further, her team will have had happy memories of the 2015 general election, when the Conservatives and Labour were, the polls attested, neck and neck (on about 34 per cent each) in the days leading up to the vote – and yet the Conservatives, much to David Cameron's enormous surprise, won with some ease, by 37.8 per cent to 31.2 per cent. So, if the polls are at times deceptive, they reckoned, then the tendency is to understate the Conservative vote quite substantially, the consequence of a phenomenon dubbed 'shy Tories'. (These were the many people who when asked which way they were voting declined to answer 'Conservative' because they were fearful of being called selfish right-wing scum by self-righteous left-wing idiots.) So the prospects couldn't have looked better, they thought.

What's more, there was a vast reservoir of UKIP votes up for grabs: the referendum had been won and so UKIP's entire raison d'être had been stripped away. Those votes would surely return to the Conservative Party. And so people were talking of a landslide victory for Theresa May, with a majority of quite possibly more than two hundred, hilarious though that might sound today. Even the less hyperbolic estimates predicted she would increase her majority to between forty and sixty seats.

This was an epic miscalculation based upon a laughably shallow reading of the political mindset of the country, false assumptions (which could have easily been tested), an underestimation of the opposition's abilities, wishful thinking and pure arrogance. It cost Theresa May her entire majority and left the government dependent upon the quixotic votes of a rump of Democratic Unionists from

Northern Ireland, a stumpy tail wagging an exhausted and increasingly fractious dog. It led us directly to where we are now, with an impasse in the House of Commons, the Prime Minister effectively hamstrung. Those problems over Northern Ireland would have been somewhat less acute, I would argue, if the Prime Minister were not utterly dependent upon the votes of the Democratic Unionist Party, which fervently opposed a hard border with Ireland.

This is not hindsight speaking. On the day that Theresa May called the election, I wrote for the *Spectator* and the *Sunday Times* that she was much more likely to lose seats than gain seats (especially in London), much to the amusement of my various colleagues who rather bought into the 'this will be a doddle' assumption. Here's why, I reckoned, the Tories had got it wrong.

First, while the national polls may have been showing large leads for the Conservatives the various recent council by-elections were showing something a little different. Here, the Tories were often losing votes to the Liberal Democrats and even Labour, especially in the north of England. It is true that people vote differently in local elections and that there is a much lower turnout, but it did strike me that the Labour vote was holding up remarkably well, north of the Severn–Trent line. The voters may have been comparatively happy with May's stewardship of the Brexit negotiations so far, but they were still not keen on austerity and nor were they keen on the Conservative Party.

Second, Labour's vote seemed to be holding firm (only two months before it had held the leaver stronghold of Stoke-on-Trent in a by-election many had predicted it would lose) at least partly because, away from Westminster, there was not remotely the same amount of animus directed towards Jeremy Corbyn as the Tories expected. Indeed, for many northern Labour voters Corbyn was certainly no worse than Ed Miliband, the previous leader. Corbyn's low personal ratings in the polls were perhaps a consequence of his relative newness and anonymity, rather than outright dislike on the part of the electorate. Labour voters in my own constituency (Middlesbrough South and East Cleveland) were actually enthusiastic that they had 'taken our party back', as they put it – away from the Blairites and Brownites who had governed it for so long.

Third, and crucially – those UKIP votes. I had a theory about this, which I tested by doing my own little bit of unscientific polling in two strongly leave-minded constituencies – Thanet South in Kent, and Hartlepool in the northeast of England – and published the outcome in the *Sunday Times*. My suspicion was that while UKIP votes in the south of the country would cheerfully transfer across to the Conservatives, they would not do so in the north.

And so as the campaigns got underway, I took myself first to Ramsgate, in South Thanet, where two years before more than 16,000 voters had put a cross beside the name of Nigel Farage. I was trying to hunt some of those voters down, which I did by asking people at random if they had voted UKIP in 2015. One middle-aged lady was appalled: 'You didn't think I was a UKIP voter did you? You need to be looking for elderly men with no teeth riding mobility scooters,' she barked – and, as it happened, she wasn't entirely wrong. I got my hundred or so – and dutifully enough, the majority said they would now be voting Conservative.

Not so at all in Hartlepool, where a sizeable proportion announced they would be voting Labour, a mystifying dozen or so Lib Dem and a few not bothering to vote at all. Away from the rural redoubts of the shires, people in the north of England (and most of the Midlands) do not like the Tories. For good reason, I might add. The consequence of this is that while the Tories would rake in lots of UKIP votes in the south, they were votes they didn't actually need, because they already held almost all of the seats. Even Nigel Farage could not prise Thanet South away from the Tories in 2015. But in the north, where they *did* need the seats, they wouldn't get them because the UKIP vote was transferring more strongly to Labour or – the point, I suppose – to absolutely anybody but the Conservatives.

Fourth, the Conservatives would lose heavily in London, partly because Corbyn's brand of intersectional agitprop infantilism plays quite well there, and partly because the Great Wen was still in deep trauma from the referendum result and still hoped that Labour might do something to reverse it. London may have been the only place in the country where Brexit was an issue at the 2017 election.

Fifth, Brenda from Bristol spoke for the vast majority of the British public. You may remember Brenda. A tidy woman in late middle age who was vox-popped on 18 April, shortly after Theresa May's announcement, by the BBC reporter Jon Kay. This is what she said when told there was to be a general election: 'You're *joking*? What, *another* one? Oh, for God's sake . . . I can't, honestly . . . I can't stand

this. There's too much politics going on at the moment . . .
why does she need to do it?' Why indeed.

Journalists excepted, the public do not like general elections. They do not like having their lives disrupted, they do
not like the rancour and the bitterness, or being barked at
and lied to and smirked at by an endless procession of
duplicitous bastards, the election dominating every news
channel, the relentless querulousness of it, the grimness.
And while they may accept the necessity once every five
years, they resent being impinged upon unnecessarily,
especially only a year after a nastily divisive referendum
and two years since the last election. When that happens,
they may be inclined to take it out on whoever called the
election, if they suspect that it might have been called not
out of necessity but simply to improve the Prime Minister's
position. '*Why* does she need to do it?' She didn't, Brenda,
but she did so anyhow. The public took note.

Sixth, the calling of the election fatally undermined
Theresa May's strongest hand as a politician. Here was a
woman, we were told, who did not play politics. She was
cut from a different kind of cloth. What she did, she did for
the good of her country (as she kept telling us), not for the
good of herself or her party. She was honest, she was
straight. After all, that's why she had resisted those calls for
a snap election: it wasn't what the country needed. After
18 April 2017, she would never quite be seen in the same
light again.

Those were the reasons, then, that I thought Theresa
May's calling of an election was a grave mistake for her, her
party and the country. And sitting there on that pleasant

spring day I reckoned to myself that she would probably lose a few seats overall, maybe five or six, just make her position slightly worse. But at that point I had yet to witness the miracle of the Conservative Party's election campaign, still less the manifesto, or bathe myself in the compelling charisma of Theresa May out on the stump . . .

9

THE 2017 CAMPAIGN

When the Labour Party announced that its MPs would respect the Brexit vote, it became clear that the 2017 general election would not be about Brexit at all, as Theresa May had seemingly intended. Indeed, Brexit scarcely figured at all during the campaign, given that the voters were left with a choice between two parties, both of which were committed to honouring the referendum result.

It should have been fertile territory, then, for the Liberal Democrats – left with that vast repository of votes from people who were opposed root and branch to Brexit. A strong Lib Dem vote would have helped the Prime Minister because the Lib Dems were expected to take votes from Labour. But the Liberal Democrat leader, Tim Farron, fought a poor campaign, most of which he spent discussing the morality, or otherwise, of buggery. A Christian who was opposed to gay marriage, the hapless Farron was repeatedly harassed by the media about his position on

homosexuality – and despite his attempts at principled
evasion on the issue almost certainly alienated a good few
Liberal Democrat votes, the party's usual supporters being
generally very much in favour of buggery and indeed
anything else that takes your fancy. That's why they're called
Liberals. And so with Brexit removed from the equation,
an already irritated public was left to look at the Conservative
Party and the Labour Party and see who offered the more
attractive future for the country, and who was the more
charismatic leader. Given what followed, this became not a
terribly hard choice.

Aside from irritating the public by calling an unwanted
election, the Conservative Party had also irritated the
Westminster hacks by telling them nothing and behaving
in a manner they considered aloof and arrogant. Disdain
for the Tories, and for Theresa May, increased every time
the Prime Minister appeared in public and delivered her
robotic message of strength, stability, certainty and so on,
with all the warmth of an Indesit fridge-freezer that had
been ineptly wired up for five quid by a man called Trevor.
It was clear immediately that May had no knack whatsoever for reaching out to the public, for selling her vision of
Britain. Nor did she have experience of doing so. May had
never run a campaign in her life: she effectively elided to
her current position. On the other hand, Jeremy Corbyn
had fought two prolonged leadership contests and won
them both and he had a competent, ruthless team behind
him – and, just as important, he was an attractive
campaigner on the stump, already transforming into what
Julie Burchill calls 'Magic Grandpa'.

In early June, the Prime Minister had consented to a cosy chat with ITV News – the polls were narrowing and this was a rather desperate attempt to sell her personality to an increasingly dubious electorate. But this was a mistake because the poor woman didn't seem to have one. It was an excruciating five minutes, within which we learned that Theresa had been 'quite shocked' at the death of her father and that the naughtiest thing she had ever done in her life was run through a cornfield when she was very young. It was, if anything, even worse than her appearance a month earlier on the BBC *One Show*, when she sat with her husband Philip and chatted in a magnificently awkward manner about who took the bins out. Theresa, apparently. But that *One Show* appearance was apt to be forgiven, however stilted and bloodless it was, because by then we hadn't seen Mrs May's manifesto and she was still well ahead in the opinion polls.

The Conservative 2017 manifesto, entitled *Forward Together*, was written by the Joint Downing Street Chief of Staff Nick Timothy and the 'promising' Conservative MP Ben Gummer, son of the not universally admired former cabinet minister to John Major and Margaret Thatcher, John Selwyn Gummer. As one cabinet minister put it to me, regarding Ben: 'Of all the fucking idiots to pick. More of a menace than anyone who has been in government in the last twenty years.' Still, Nick and Ben were so utterly delighted with their manifesto that they decided not to show it to anybody at all until one day before its release to the public, and this included members of the cabinet, one of whom had seen the manifesto only half an hour before he was due to introduce the Prime Minister to read from it. But Nick and Tim were convinced it was a real winner. That was a mistake. Nick resigned from his position at Downing Street the morning after the election and now writes for the *Daily Telegraph*. Ben Gummer lost his seat in Ipswich where Labour increased its share of the vote by more than 10 per cent, much to the enormous delight of many of his former Conservative colleagues. I have no idea what he's doing now. One Conservative backbencher remarked that he would never be allowed to be an MP again, having orches- trated a campaign in which so many Tories lost their seats. That's how good a manifesto it was.

The headlines from this forlorn document? In the open- ing section, the Prime Minister told us that she preferred 'strong and stable' leadership, which came as an enormous surprise. But what was she offering a public that was by now tired of austerity and perhaps hankering for a fairer Britain?

1. A plan to end free lunches for infant school children (OK, some would get breakfasts instead);
2. taking winter fuel payments away from lots of old people because they could afford to live without them;
3. taking the homes away from people with dementia so that they could pay for their own care;
4. ending the triple lock on pensions and replacing it with a double lock.

Whoever thought that those first three policies would appeal to the electorate was presumably in the early stages of the affliction mentioned in point 3. Meanwhile, as regards number 4, only twenty-three people in the entire United Kingdom knew the difference between a triple-locked and double-locked pension.

But it was the so-called dementia tax that really frightened the voters. As the *Spectator*'s James Forsyth put it, Tory voters had hitherto considered Theresa May to be 'one of their own' and would always protect property ownership, perhaps above all else. But here she was insisting that, if you went doolally, your home, if it was worth more than £100,000, would be sequestered to pay for someone to look after you in your drooling mania. The Conservative Party has traditionally looked after the old, not least for reasons of self-interest (the older you are, the more likely you are to vote Conservative). And here they were sticking it to property owners and the elderly. A double whammy.

But there was more to come. Buried away in a section entitled 'Stronger Communities' and under the subheading 'Our Countryside Communities' was a pledge to have a go at overturning the ban on hunting foxes with hounds. This was picked up by the media very quickly indeed. Tories to have a new vote on fox-hunting! I had been preparing to vote Conservative for the first time in my life when I read this and decided, immediately, not to. But you don't have to be as viscerally and implacably opposed to blood sports as I am to understand the political stupidity of such a pledge. The ban on fox-hunting is one of the most popular pieces of legislation passed in the last three decades and the last opinion poll on the issue showed that 85 per cent of people agreed with it, and a hefty proportion actually wanted the law strengthened (reasonably enough, as the hunters still get away with hunting foxes). Pretty much the only people in favour of repealing the Hunting Act were already Tory voters. What possibly did Theresa May have to gain by making such a pledge? Perhaps Timothy and Gummer felt that it was not a big issue on the doorsteps and that it might serve as a useful sop to Conservative Party activists. But, believe me, it is an issue on the doorsteps. As I trudged around northern constituencies asking voters about the election, the two things I heard most often were: 'She's going to take my house away when I go mental!' and 'They're going to start ripping foxes to bits again!' Especially, in both cases, from female voters.

What a dismal menu to put before the electorate and what an impoverished vision of Britain. Meanness towards the young and the elderly – and let's kill some wild animals. Oh, and a few quid bunged to the NHS, which every party promises at every election. It was a manifesto devoid of imagination and which, crucially, lacked an understanding of the lives of 'ordinary' people, their hopes and aspirations. Perhaps this is because Timothy and Gummer felt there was no need to offer an attractive vision, for the votes were already in the bag. More arrogance and complacency again, you might argue. It was, according to several backbenchers, the worst Conservative manifesto in a hundred years and worse still, as it transpired, the votes certainly were not in the bag. The 'naive' (according to one senior Conservative politician I spoke to) assumption was that with a 21 per cent lead to play with, the government could for once afford to put forward 'difficult' (i.e. unpopular) policies that it would then be compelled, because they were manifesto commitments, to see through both the House of Commons and the House of Lords.

Neither Gummer nor the bright and capable Timothy had experience of running campaigns and those who did have experience were excluded from the decision-making. Quite often when manifestos are published the senior MPs, including the frontbench, discover one or two things with which they disagree and within a few days these quibbles bubble up to the surface. Not with this. 'On day one, as soon as we read it it was . . . what the *fuck*?' one senior minister told me. Another commented: 'I literally did not believe what I was reading.'

The first consequence of the manifesto was to sap the strength and belief from leading figures within the Conservative Party, who were now dispatched to the TV and radio studios to explain the triple-lock pension stuff, or persuade people that the demented needed their homes taking off them. They did so with growing despair and, in some cases, fury. The Conservative Party is ever prone to convenient disunity, and the manifesto allowed that disunity to surface. Cabinet ministers complained to the Prime Minister, but to no apparent avail. There was dissent in the ranks, and that dissent would stay for the following eighteen months.

The next consequence of the manifesto was to alienate the public, who had already been wondering what they had been called out to vote for. This? This is it?

The Labour manifesto was already out. Entitled *For the Many Not the Few*, the foreword by Magic Grandpa exhorted: 'Let's build a fairer Britain where no one is held back. A country where everybody is able to get on in life, to have security at work and at home, to be decently paid for the work they do, and to live their lives with the dignity they deserve.'

Platitudinous, perhaps, but attractive platitudes none-theless. And Labour was offering thirty hours of free child care for everyone (quite possibly also for people who didn't have children), the renationalisation of the energy compan-ies, water companies, Royal Mail and rail services (all popular with the voters, according to the polls), to be paid for by a tax on rich bastards, so to speak. This was good, left-wing populism – and it clearly struck a chord. How it would be costed was a different matter, but nobody was terribly concerned about that.

The combination of rich-bashing (which included a tax on the City of London's financial institutions) with lavish handouts to 'the many' and the promise of lower energy costs and an end to austerity would have sounded, to many working-class voters as well as the 'squeezed middle', like manna from heaven in comparison. The Conservative manifesto offered nothing. And as the Maybot continued to intone, like a Chatty Cathy doll programmed by the world's most boring insurance salesman, 'strength and stability', over and over, the public began to discern that even those two qualities might well be missing from the Prime Minister's personality, given the evident and grow-ing disunity in the ranks and her increasingly ashen facade. There was a certain feeling, too, that May's perpetual mantra was the opposite of what many wanted: they desired change.

The polls narrowed, ominously. Nobody talked about majorities of two hundred any more, or even of a hundred. And yet the polls were still seriously underestimating the Labour vote: they had got it badly wrong again, for the third time in succession. On the eve of the vote an IPSOS Mori poll put the Conservatives 8 points ahead, while a BMG poll suggested the lead was 13 per cent. If you believed the polls, the Tories were home and dry. But the polls are never right these days.

And so on the morning of 9 June we awoke to the by now familiar sight of David Dimbleby looking rather discombobulated and the in-house pollsters attempting to disguise, once again, their utter mystification. The Conservatives had taken 43.5 per cent, the Labour Party 41 per cent, a percentage lead reduced almost tenfold from the opinion poll positions back in the first week of May. More to the point, the Conservative Party had lost thirteen seats and with them their entire majority. They now had 317 seats in parliament, having needed 326 for an overall majority. The Labour Party gained thirty seats, while the Liberal Democrats – incredibly, as they were the only major party to be unequivocally against Brexit – saw their vote reduce by 0.5 per cent and, in one of the few moments of cheer, the former leader Nick Clegg lost his seat in Sheffield Hallam.

For the analysts, the headline story was of a return to two-party politics: Labour and the Conservatives took a higher proportion of the vote than at any time since 1970 (which was another occasion, now I think of it, when the pollsters got it completely wrong). I have heard it said, many times, that one reason for the higher than expected

Labour vote was that people thought they could put their cross beside Magic Grandpa's party knowing that they would not get in, so as a kind of protest vote. I don't buy that argument, largely because the precise converse of that thesis was used to explain the failure of UKIP to gain parliamentary seats at elections, i.e. that lots of people wouldn't vote for them because they thought they stood no chance of winning. You surely cannot have it both ways.

May was forced to try to cobble together a minority government with Arlene Foster's ten Democratic Unionist Party MPs. During the ghastly election campaign, Theresa May had rather patronisingly lectured a nurse who was demanding more money for the NHS with the words 'there is no magic money tree'. Ah, but there was – and only a few days later Theresa found it, gave it a bit of a shake and out dropped a handy £1 billion bung to secure the coalition deal with the DUP. Being dependent upon this rump of peremptorily purchased Ulster politicians led directly to the problems that the government has experienced over the Northern Ireland backstop, the most serious impediment to a Brexit deal.

But it was much worse than that. With May's majority evaporated, she lost enormous clout in her negotiations with the EU, which now knew it was dealing with a government whose position was excruciatingly precarious and, better still, a Conservative Party in parliament that was divided straight down the middle. It strengthened the hands of Michel Barnier and Jean-Claude Juncker enormously. It strengthened the hand of the more extreme remainer Conservative MPs too, enabling them to hold the government to ransom whenever they wished. It diminished the standing of the Prime Minister in the eyes of her party and the eyes of the electorate: no longer could she use the phrase 'strong and stable' without people laughing hysterically. She had run a presidential-style election campaign but looked a million miles from being presidential. She had infuriated her backbenchers and a large proportion of her cabinet. She was forced to crawl before the 1922 Committee and apologise.

'If you want to zero in on one thing which damaged our negotiating abilities, it was the election and particularly the manifesto,' one former cabinet minister told me. A case of ineptitude and arrogance, a lethal combination.

Oh – I just found out what Ben Gummer is doing today. He's a 'senior advisor' to the management consultancy firm, McKinsey. I hope they pay well for his important advice.

10

NEGOTIATIONS I

At 4.10 in the morning of 8 December 2017, the official limousines pulled up outside 10 Downing Street. Five minutes later Theresa May and her Brexit Secretary, David Davis, clambered inside the cars, with their retinue of various spads – special advisors – and civil servants. They had been summoned, you see. Summoned to Brussels by an unelected official of the European Union: Jean-Claude Juncker, the Luxembourgish President of the European Commission. When an unelected panjandrum like Juncker summons you, you move. You climb out of bed two hours before dawn, swill down some coffee and get in the car. You do as you are told. It doesn't matter that you are the Prime Minister of the United Kingdom and the unelected official is a preening, smug bureaucrat from a microstate who is allegedly often worse for wear (if you get my meaning). You are at his beck and call – *4.10 in the morning, no problem sir!* You may glean from this small vignette where the power lay in negotiations between the UK and the EU. It did not seem to lie in 10 Downing Street.

What follows is a summary of why the British position was fatally weakened in our negotiations with the European Union team, in no particular order. It does not go into the detail of those negotiations – that will follow.

1. The Prime Minister herself did not wish to leave the European Union, and nor did nearly half of her cabinet and perhaps any of the civil servants who accompanied both her and whatever Brexit Secretary was in situ at a given time. In other words, no matter what statements of strength and stability issued from the British side, the EU knew they were dealing with a divided country, a divided government and a Prime Minister who thought it much better that Britain remain within the EU, no matter what she said at the table. This was an enormous psychological advantage for the EU negotiators. Further, the EU team was for once – 'uniquely', as Jochen Buchsteiner from the *Frankfurter Allgemeine Zeitung* put it – both united and focused on very clear goals. And so too were the twenty-seven countries of the EU.

2. The Prime Minister herself was the Chief Negotiator, as she informed each of the Brexit secretaries who, one after another, resigned because they felt that she was conceding too much to Brussels. In theory, this is right and proper: she was, after all, the Prime Minister. But it ignores Theresa May's abilities, or

lack of abilities, in the business of haggling. As a popular meme had it at the time, 'Theresa May was the kind of negotiator to come out of DFS with a full-priced sofa.' The country had witnessed Theresa May's selling skills only a few weeks before negotiations began, in the general election during which she managed to persuade an unexpectedly sizeable proportion of the electorate that they would be much better off voting for Jeremy Corbyn.

3. The British civil service was a particular problem: it was, from the start, obvious that it was not neutral on the issue of the UK leaving the EU, as both cabinet ministers and Conservative backbenchers told me. Further, the PM's team were – in the words of one former cabinet minister – 'essentially the same fucking crowd who had handled David Cameron's visit to Brussels in early 2016 and come away with nothing'. The distance between what the politicians wanted and what the civil servants thought they should get was made plain by the resignation letter to staff of the UK's EU Ambassador Sir Ivan Rogers: 'I hope you will continue to challenge ill-founded arguments and muddled thinking and that you will never be afraid to speak the truth to those in power. I hope that you will support each other in those difficult moments where you have to deliver messages that are disagreeable to those who need to hear them.' He also insisted that the ministers needed to hear some 'hard truths' from the other side of the table. On March 10, 2019, the

Sunday Times reported the views of a pro-leave civil servant. This is what the anonymous informant had to say about the supposedly neutral civil service's attitude to Brexit: 'It has become clear to me that the vast majority of civil servants support "remain". From my own observations I would estimate this number to be well over 90%. This is worrying in itself and far from representative of the 52% of the population who voted for Brexit.

Most horrifying, however, is the sheer disdain and utter contempt that my colleagues display towards people who voted to leave. I have lost count of the number of insulting and derogatory terms that are used in my own department and elsewhere to refer to the 17.4m people who voted for Brexit: "racist", "stupid", "uneducated". Anti-Brexit jokes and snide remarks are dropped casually into everyday office conversations . . .

'. . . This entire culture creates a thickening cloud of negativity towards Brexit that shades all areas of the civil service. I have witnessed first-hand civil servants doing everything within their power, subtly and under the surface, to frustrate Brexit and talk it down at every opportunity. This can only seriously undermine our efforts to be in the strongest position possible on leaving the EU.'

4. Theresa May signed the letter giving official notice under Article 50 of the Lisbon Treaty on 29 March 2017 and it was delivered to Donald Tusk, President of the European Council, a day later. Negotiations

were due to start shortly afterwards, and indeed there were a couple of preliminary meetings in April – however, the real business was postponed because within two weeks of 29 March Theresa May called a general election. At the time she did so she had a workable, if not convincing, majority of seventeen. She had called the election to increase her majority and show her strength as a leader to both the country and the EU. When the proper negotiations started on 19 June, her majority had been wiped out and her government was dependent upon a minority regional party for its continued existence. Her strength, then, had been considerably lessened and close to destroyed. Further, the appalling election result left her perpetually attempting to square the circle between her remainer MPs and the more hardline Brexiteers in her party, a circle that could never truly be squared and which led to vacillations and climb downs in her discussions with Brussels.

5. While the Prime Minister, who had voted remain, led the discussions, she did so in consultation with her Brexit Secretaries, who were all pro-leave. It is clear, then, that before each round of negotiations, the Prime Minister was forced to negotiate with her own side. As one former Brexit Secretary told me, the two would discuss the various components of forthcoming negotiations and 'agree on perhaps two-thirds of them, until they crossed one of our red lines'. What then followed would be either a fudge or one of the two parties (PM and Brexit Secretary)

entering negotiations based upon policies upon which they fundamentally disagreed.

6. The Brexit Secretaries, and especially David Davis, entered negotiations with a priority to concentrate on 'the big picture', rather than to be immersed in detail. To pretty much the same extent this was true of Michel Barnier and Donald Tusk on the EU side as well. This meant that the fine detail was left to the civil servants on both sides. The problem here is that with EU law, the fine detail determined the big picture and not the other way about. The British side was thus too often left a fait accompli to crucial detail that had been agreed between the two teams of civil servants who, one assumes, largely agreed with each other.

7. Theresa May and the British side serially underestimated the EU's desire – and indeed *need* – to punish the UK as a deterrent to other countries that might have been thinking of getting out, and thus displaying to the rest of Europe an intransigence and implacability, whereas the Brits seemed to assume that negotiations would have about them a certain consensuality founded on the basis that the EU needed a decent deal with the UK to preserve its own export market, etc. May and her team were too slow to understand the hostility, and yet they had been given every indication that this was precisely what would happen. On 30 March 2017, the European Parliament's representative to the Brexit negotiations, the liberal Belgian MEP Guy

Verhofstadt, said: 'Britain has shot itself in the foot. We intend to shoot you in the other.' That seems to me a decent indication of what the British might expect. On the same day the Dutch Prime Minister Mark Rutte demanded that the British be 'brought back to earth' and that Theresa May's aspirations for Brexit were 'Alice in Wonderland' and 'totally unrealistic'. This was before negotiations had even properly begun.

8. Paradoxically, it might seem, the British were also too slow to understand that the EU side was very anxious, on occasion, to reach agreement, despite the rhetoric and the unpleasant asides from the likes of Jean-Claude Juncker and Donald Tusk that followed, invariably, every round of negotiation. Time and again, faced with the prospect of a failed negotiation and no agreement, the EU side would quietly shift ground, urged all the while to do so by either the business lobby in Europe or indeed some of the elected politicians of the twenty-seven European countries, France and Ireland excepted. There was a divide between what the EU bureaucrats wanted and what the governments and industries in Europe wanted. This division was not exploited by the British.

9. Theresa May's most crucial bargaining chip – we will leave with no deal – was rendered impotent by the actions of members of her own cabinet and especially the Chancellor of the Exchequer. The correct approach to negotiations would have been

to explain to Barnier et al. at the outset: 'We are leaving the EU. We are perfectly happy to do so with no
deal other than a WTO deal, and pay you nothing
whatsoever. But you are our friends and allies and
we would like to be helpful . . .' But May could
scarcely use the threat of no deal – which would be
gravely injurious to countries within the EU –
because the threat was palpably false. At various
stages, over the course of eighteen months, when
May and her team left for negotiations, Philip
Hammond, the Chancellor, would state either that
there was no possibility of a no-deal Brexit, or that a
no-deal Brexit would mean 'planes won't be able to
take off', or that the economy would be ruined.
Fellow front-bench remainers echoed these remarks
and added a few of their own. Seen from the EU
perspective, this made it clear that 'no deal' was a
paper tiger when it should have been the starting
point from which negotiations proceeded – and, of
course, Hammond should have been sacked. In
short, May's strongest weapon was effectively taken
away from her. Look at the speed with which the EU
began to shift a little, in early 2019, when it appeared
that no deal might be the consequence purely
through default (i.e. running out of time). But even
then members of her own parliamentary party were
attempting to make clear to the EU that this denouement simply would not be allowed to happen.

10. The divorce bill – whatever it was to be – should
have been left to the very end of negotiations. The

threat being: if we leave with no deal at all, you get nothing. The bill itself was concocted in much the same way as the bill for an ice cream and a cup of coffee tends to be concocted by Venetian café owners when they have just received a party of middle-aged American tourists. It had scant basis in fact, as you could see from the vast differences in the amounts that the EU wanted to charge us. Some £85 billion, according to the French. Rather less, according to the Germans. Given that the total amount of money we have paid into the EU since 1973 is only £187 billion, these sums bandied about by the EU seem to me devoid of a sense of reality. The problem was, however, that we once again began negotiating from their position, when there was no need.

11. Following on from my last point, Theresa May's hands were bound from the outset because we conceded too much on the *sequencing* of the matters · to be discussed. Put very coarsely, we committed ourselves from day one to a programme that began with what *we* would have to concede to *them* – and only at the end of that, when the bill had been drawn up, would the UK get the chance to negotiate the trade deals it wanted. In short, we followed the EU's agenda and were perpetually at the EU's beck and call.

12. The Prime Minister was too worried about parliamentary numbers back home. She was terrified that too intransigent a disposition towards the EU would inflame her remainer colleagues, or that a

concession here or there would provoke an angry reaction from the European Research Group of pro-Brexit MPs. In a sense this was simply a failure of leadership; carry the country with you and the numbers will tend to follow. But that chutzpah was never present.

Not all of these things are Theresa May's fault, of course – and it is true that some are offered here with the great benefit of hindsight. The Prime Minister was the prisoner of unfortunate circumstances – even if those were horrible circumstances that she skilfully created for herself.

11

NEGOTIATIONS II

The Prime Minister's formal letter of withdrawal from the European Union, written on 29 March 2017, contained seven proposals for how negotiations should proceed. The very first proposal was this: '[for] engaging with one another constructively and respectfully, in a spirit of sincere cooperation'. Call me a cynic, but I'm not 100 per cent convinced that the European Union abided by that injunction. What that first letter should also have outlined, but did not, was a polite insistence that talks on trade should come first, or at least run in parallel with those issues which the EU wished to address. Meanwhile the EU had been insistent from the very start that trade agreements were not on the agenda until they had got what *they* wanted. As discussed, the UK followed the EU's sequencing of negotiations almost without demurral: it was an early and crucial victory for Tusk and Barnier.

And yet while the UK obediently followed the EU's timetabling, it seemed to lose grasp of a sense of principle on one of the very first issues to be discussed, which was the status of UK citizens living abroad and EU citizens living in the UK. Here, for once, the UK was playing hard-ball, much to the understandable distress and panic of the millions of EU citizens living in Great Britain and to the – again, understandable – fury of especially the liberal media at home. The principled response would have been to unilaterally and immediately guarantee the rights and tenure of all EU citizens living in the UK, because indi-vidual citizens should surely never be used as bargaining chips. If the EU wishes to go down that route, regarding UK citizens living among the other twenty-seven member states, then let them. And so let the world see on what side lay the rectitude and moral decency. That they did not do so, and instead left our migrant workers in limbo for several months, was perhaps a consequence of Conservative misapprehension over the British public's attitude to immigration. There was no hostility in the UK towards the actual immigrants from EU countries, merely a worry that too many were coming in and were under-cutting the wages of low-skilled Brits. The same misap-prehension had surfaced earlier, while David Cameron was Prime Minister, with plans to deprive new arrivals of their benefits for a certain period. This was unjust and cruel and perhaps the result of the Tories swallowing the liberal line that those people opposed to immigration must be racist and feel ill-disposed towards the immi-grants themselves. It was as late as January 2019 that the Prime Minister scrapped her proposed, mean-spirited charge of £65 to be paid by every EU citizen who wished to continue living in the UK, the deal for them to do so having at last been struck.

The first thing the EU wanted was money, as much as possible, predicated upon the supposition that the UK had been a party to future EU spending proposals and commitments and could not now simply renege on them. If the UK owed anything at all to the EU – and there is good reason to suggest that it owes not a single penny – the means for calculating that cost vary from country to country and are in any case purely hypothetical. A House of Lords report from early March 2017, well before negotiations began, ventured that the UK might owe nothing at all and added: 'even if it were to be accepted that the UK had any financial liability on leaving the EU, no single figure can incontrovertibly represent an amount that the UK might be requested to pay.' Indeed, as I mentioned, the figures were wildly divergent depending upon what part of the EU you talked to. Seemingly ignored altogether were the monies that the UK might justifiably claim back from the EU. For example, the EU itself has assets of £154 billion and, based upon the UK's contributions, which amount to 15 per cent of the EU's budget, we might usefully have demanded somewhere in the region of £23 billion upon our exit from the EU. And that's before we look at the assets owned by the European Investment Bank, within which the UK was of course a stakeholder. The House of Lords advised that we might be able to trouser something like £3 billion as a consequence.

Yet in signing up to discussing our divorce bill at the outset and with a necessarily finite time limit on negotiations, the pressure was on the UK to succumb to this institutionalised embezzlement – so that we might at some point get around to talks on trade. We capitulated on the principle very early and have agreed to bunging them something in the region of £36 billion, although the final figure still has to be determined. That £36 billion seems to me a little steep.

But what was happening on the politically difficult issues – our relationship with the EU's Customs Union, our attempts to wriggle free of the European Court of Justice (ECJ) and, of course, the vexed problem of Northern Ireland? To take the ECJ first, even the most impassioned remainer would surely concede that in voting to leave the EU, we had voted to free ourselves from its dominion, its presiding over us. Without any question that meant freeing ourselves *entirely* from the ECJ. This was certainly the intention of the British negotiating team in the autumn of 2017 – but following that, as often happens, winter set in.

Once again, the EU called the shots, this time summoning the Prime Minister to a lunch with Jean-Claude Juncker, the President of the European Commission, where the fine detail about our relationship with the ECJ – and decisions over Northern Ireland – would be thrashed out. The lunch was to take place on 4 December and, on the day before, Theresa May spoke to her Brexit Secretary, David Davis, and informed him that her team had decided the wording for the agreements, and that was that. This was No. 10 effectively taking over the negotiations and it marked the start of the bizarre process by which two successive leave-minded Brexit Secretaries were largely cut out of the decision-making process, forced to be accomplices to agreements with which they fundamentally disagreed and which would lead in both cases – Davis and his successor, Dominic Raab – to their resignations.

What happened on the weekend leading up to that lunch was that the Prime Minister and the No. 10 team 'lost their nerve', as it was put to me. Perpetually worried about the numbers back in the House of Commons and the disposition of her querulous pro-remain MPs, and propelled towards a set of agreements that Brussels was anxious to secure, the Prime Minister gave away far too much. The agreement on the continued role of the ECJ was an obvious sticking point for anyone who had voted leave. The government signed up to a stipulation that: 'The CJEU [or ECJ] is the ultimate arbiter of the interpretation of European law. In the context of the application or interpretation of those rights, UK courts shall therefore have due regard to relevant decisions of the CJEU after the specified date' – the specified date being withdrawal. In fact, the agreement made provisions for the ECJ to continue being an 'ultimate arbiter' for at least eight years following our withdrawal, and arguably indefinitely.

Still more ground was ceded on the issue of Northern Ireland. According to an insider the Prime Minister had been desperately calling the Irish Taoiseach, Leo Varadkar, at every available moment during the three days that preceded her lunch with Juncker et al. – but he didn't pick up the phone and refused to return any of her calls. She had been anxious to strike some kind of deal. In the end, over that lunch, she conceded that Northern Ireland would be in full alignment with the Republic of Ireland, meaning harmonisation with the EU on matters of trade and therefore an immediate conflict with the Good Friday Agreement with regard to the notion of an 'all island economy'.

The Irish were absolutely delighted, of course. But the Northern Irish were not. Halfway through her lunch with Juncker, May was disturbed from her mussels and chips (or whatever) by the shrill and insistent ringing of her mobile phone. It was Arlene Foster, the leader of the Democratic Ulster Unionists, and May's 'confidence and supply' partner in what was effectively a coalition. Foster told her that the deal she was about to strike was totally unacceptable and would lose her the support not only of the DUP but many of her own pro-Brexit backbenchers, who indeed immediately convened a meeting to express their staunch opposition and were, by the end of it, unanimous in their utter disdain. The former First Minister of Northern Ireland, David (now Lord) Trimble, commented that the agreement was 'minted in Dublin' and would appal all unionists north of the border. In practice it separated Northern Ireland from the rest of the UK and tied it closely not simply to the EU, but to Ireland. Often a sticking point, for the unionists, that one.

The Juncker lunch perhaps marked the beginning of the time at which No. 10 began to pursue an alternative Brexit strategy to the one agreed in cabinet, and thus became separated by an ever-increasing distance from the aspirations of pro-Brexit ministers. David Davis, still clinging on as Brexit Secretary at this point, puts the date rather later – the meeting at Chequers in February 2018 – at which Theresa May's team began to formulate an alternative strategy in tandem with that agreed by cabinet. But the beginnings of this process were there at that Juncker lunch in December 2017. From that moment on, until the second – and crucial – Chequers meeting of 6 July 2018, Davis more and more disagreed with the Prime Minister over negotiating strategy, seeing red lines being crossed almost every time they spoke. He remained in office, however, although throughout the spring and early summer there were rumours that he was about to resign (which he denied).

Friday 6 July, 2018. Sultry and windless. By lunchtime in the Chilterns the temperature was over 30 °C. The cabinet turned up to the sixteenth-century pile in the relative cool of morning. And when they arrived at the front door they were told that their mobile phones were to be confiscated, much as a junior school teacher might do to an unruly class of eight-year-olds. This was presumably to prevent them from tweeting disparaging remarks about how the discussions were going. The politicians were also told that if they didn't sign up to the deal about to be put before them, they ought to order taxis to take them home because they would no longer be cabinet ministers and would thus be deprived of their ministerial transport. David Davis, already knowing he was dead meat, half thought of ringing Jacob Rees-Mogg and requesting that he might swing by and pick him up in his Bentley – which, he reckoned, would have a certain fuck-you grandeur about it. But he couldn't because he no longer had a phone.

The plan put before the cabinet that day – a hundred pages long with a three-page summary – was excruciatingly poor, a mish-mash of wishful thinking, woeful

compromise and in truth a substantial reneging on the
decision taken by the British electorate. It left the UK tied,
in perpetuity, to the EU's customs tariffs but, of course
being outside the EU, without the influence we had when
we were a member state. It was worse than a no-deal Brexit
and worse than staying within the EU. Even the EU hated
it. So did everybody else: the Prime Minister had confected
this deal in an attempt to unite her two warring tribes
within government, the leavers and remainers. In this she
was spectacularly successful – each side found it as risible a
deal as the other.

And yet the Chequers meeting ended with a display of
unity by the entire cabinet and much platitudinous talk of
optimism and moving forwards. The Foreign Secretary,
Boris Johnson, even made what was described as a 'moving'
speech in support of the plan. Within a matter of days he
was to liken it to a roll of lavatory paper, a suicide vest
wrapped around the British constitution, a semi-Brexit,
utterly feeble, and the reduction of Britain to the status of a
vassal state. 'At every stage of the talks so far, Brussels gets
what Brussels wants,' he complained. 'It is a humiliation.
We look like a seven-stone weakling being comically bent
out of shape by a 500lb gorilla.'

Johnson resigned three days after Chequers and the post
of Foreign Secretary went to another remainer, the former
Health Secretary Jeremy Hunt. Brexiteer influence upon
the government was waning daily. Meanwhile, that Friday,
after the joint declaration of unanimous support for this
dog's breakfast of a plan, the Brexit Secretary David Davis
took advantage of still being in post by taking his

ministerial limo home from Buckinghamshire – or, rather, to the pad of the former chief whip Andrew Mitchell, where he crashed for the night to avoid being doorstepped by the hacks next morning. He bided his time for a day and then resigned from the cabinet on the morning of Sunday 8 July. Three months later he drafted a letter to his fellow MPs in which he ripped the Chequers deal apart: 'The Chequers deal fails to take back control of our laws, money, borders and trade because it proposes a common rulebook, a facilitated customs arrangement and effective subordination to the European Court of Justice. That was always unacceptable as it does not meet the requirements of the referendum or our subsequent promises to the electorate.'

By then, mind, the European Union had already rejected – unanimously, almost out of hand – the Chequers deal for very different reasons, largely over the failure to provide a backstop plan for Northern Ireland and thus the borders between the UK and the EU. Davis insisted, in his letter, that the stark choice offered by May – it's either no deal or this deal – was very far from the truth.

But the truth had receded a little from the minds of many of those people charged with delivering Brexit. Theresa May was now caught up in a process that in the end obscured the point of the exercise. From here on in the tail began to wag the dog. The point now for May, however much she insisted her goal was to deliver what the people had asked for, was instead to ensure that her government survived. It meant treading an increasingly hazardous line between squaring what her remainers, in cabinet and outside, wanted and what the Brexiteers were demanding.

And the problem for May is that this was a circle that could never possibly be squared. You cannot be both inside a club and outside it; some issues have about them a Manichean divide, and this is one of them. In short, she was left scuttling to Brussels and back attempting to placate two sides who wanted diametrically opposite things, balancing in her mind the precarious arithmetic of her majority. This led directly to the farcical, multiple impasses of December 2018 and winter and spring 2019 and the point, at last, when it became clear that Brexit simply wasn't going to happen.

12

THE ERG

They meet every Tuesday evening at six o'clock in a committee room at the House of Commons. Sometimes fifty or sixty strong, occasionally swelled to well over a hundred by the peers who are also allowed to shuffle along, when the mood, when the imperative, takes them.

They are united in a belief that we should leave the European Union and also, more recently, in a kind of seething loathing of the former Prime Minister. 'The duplicity of the woman is amazing' and 'she is completely fucking mendacious' were just two of the observations made to me by members of this cabal. This dangerous cabal, if you are to believe their colleagues in the House of Commons and the liberal commentators. Hardline Brexiteers. Right-wing extremists. Actually 'worse than neo-Nazis' according to Labour MP, David Lammy.

They are led by their elected chairman, Jacob Rees-Mogg, a charming Edwardian anachronism, and five officers from within the party. Boris Johnson, David Davis and Michael Gove are regular attendees: this grouping does not have membership, per se, just a sense of affiliation. Within the Conservative Party in parliament they number perhaps eighty MPs at best. Along with the ten Democratic Unionist politicians and a handful of brave Labour recusants on Europe – Kate Hoey, John Mann, Frank Field, Gisela Stuart and so on – they comprise the entire total of MPs within the House who were pro-Brexit before the referendum, i.e. politicians who are really pro-Brexit, rather than simply insisting to the world that the decision of the electorate must be respected while doing everything they possibly can to undermine that decision. As such, then, they are outnumbered in Parliament by about six to one.

Whatever criticisms I make of them then, in the following, should be mitigated by that fact. If they have not always been united on what to do it has tended to be the consequence of a divide between those who believe in the art of the possible, given such parliamentary opposition to their beliefs, and those who cleave to the piety of a Brexit that the people of Britain voted for. Not a soft Brexit, or a Brexit with a semi lob on, just a Brexit: freedom from the European Union and its institutions and machinations. They have not always played their cards terribly well, for sure. There is evidence, to my mind, of a certain delusion among some of its members. They have been comprehensively wrong-footed time and again by the Prime Minister and deliberately deprived of knowledge of what the government is up to at any moment in time. But hell, they tried. You have to say that. They tried.

The European Research Group (ERG) was founded by the former Conservative MP for West Worcestershire, Michael Spicer (now Lord Spicer), back in 1993, primarily in response to the signing of the Maastricht Treaty – which is seen by the ERG, perhaps rightly, as the dark origin of most of our current ills and is certainly the point at which the Conservative Party became irrevocably split on the issue of the EU. Maastricht was signed by the European Economic Community leaders in early 1992 and its first act was to remove the word 'Economic' from the EEC: this was no longer a simple trading organisation, a kind of updated Hanseatic League, but had much higher aspirations indeed. These included a common foreign and security policy and also 'cooperation' over justice and home affairs. It also paved the way for the creation of a single European currency, the euro.

Maastricht's popularity with the people of Europe, as opposed to the politicians running it, was questionable. Three countries offered their citizens a referendum. In France, the treaty sneaked by with the narrowest of margins, just 50.8 per cent being in favour. However, there were no cavils from the establishment about the narrowness of this support for major constitutional change, or suggestions that there should be a second vote just to clear things up a bit, or that the poll wasn't binding. The Danes also held a referendum and voted against Maastricht. But having been given a few placatory sops to cheer them up they were of course marched back down to the polling stations again and told to get it right this time, which they did.

There was no referendum in the UK, despite there being arguably a good constitutional reason for one. What way would the Brits have voted? It is pretty certain they would have been against. Throughout the mid-1990s opinion polls on the European Union tended to show two things.

First, that most of the time British people wished to remain members of the EC or EEC – and sometimes by a large majority. Second, that all successive attempts by the EC to extend its remit were met with strong popular opposition. Let me give you two examples of this. There was not a single opinion poll within the entire decade (1990s) that showed a majority of British people in favour of ditching the pound and joining the single European currency: not one. This was despite the fact that the three major parties were either partly or wildly in favour and that we were already, for a while, part of the EC's Exchange Rate Mechanism, designed to harmonise currencies across the bloc.

Second, when plans were announced for a series of referendums across Europe on adopting a single European Union constitution in the early years of this century, an idea much approved of by our then Prime Minister Tony Blair, opinion poll support for this notion stood at just 27 per cent in the UK. Blair dropped plans for the referendum and indeed referenda were cancelled across the continent given the microscopic support for a joint constitution Europewide (apart from in Luxembourg, natch). The EU decided instead to pursue a constitution by stealth or diktat, rather than involving the general public – who are so often on these occasions inclined to be terribly unhelpful. Still, the British public's view was much then as it is today: we would like to be part of a European trading bloc, but nothing much more than that, thank you.

Maastricht left a corrosive divide within the Conservative Party and pointed towards a still greater divide in the country, partly between the people and the elite, also between those who were happy for greater integration and the European project and those who were not. As ever, while the weight of numbers was on the side that resisted the creation of a federal European superstate, the balance of power always resided with those who were not remotely averse to it. So, a year later, Michael Spicer formed the ERG: Bill Cash, now Sir William Cash, was an early supporter. So too was the former Prime Minister, Margaret Thatcher ('I would never have signed that treaty,' she said of Maastricht). And, irony of ironies, the current speaker of the House of Commons John Bercow. Some MPs left the Conservative party altogether and joined Sir James Goldsmith's Referendum Party, which campaigned for the UK to leave the EC or EU, as it became. Some later joined the embryonic United Kingdom Independence Party. The majority of dissidents – the Maastricht Rebels – remained within the fold, however, and bedevilled John Major's singularly inept and fragile government until its inevitable defeat in 1997 to a youthful and smirking Tony Blair.

So, six o'clock in that fusty if spacious committee room. The ERG saw its task as to hold the Prime Minister to account over Brexit, and given the parlous nature of her majority and the presence within May's cabinet of several

ERG supporters, at first it had a certain leverage in so doing. Until MV2, perhaps. Until then. In November 2018 Theresa May returned from Brussels with a deal, 'May's Deal', which she had agreed with Barnier, Tusk et al. A vote was to be held in parliament on 11 December and gradually details of the 500-plus-page document became evident, especially the critical stuff – about the Northern Ireland backstop. May's deal, it became clear, effectively separated Northern Ireland from the rest of the United Kingdom, leaving it tied to the EU for an unspecified period of time. Further, the backstop meant that the UK would be forced to remain within the EU's Customs Union for an unspecified period of time and to some extent would also be under the jurisdiction of the European Commission and the European Court of Justice – indefinitely. Even worse, the UK could not scrap the backstop unilaterally: it needed the agreement of the European Union to do so.

This is obviously not what was meant by Brexit and it became patent there and then that the deal would be heavily defeated if it went ahead to a vote on 11 December. Plenty of remainers were against it, too, on the grounds that it left the UK in a much worse position regarding the EU than either a no deal, on World Trade Organization terms, or remaining within the EU. She cancelled the vote the day before it was due to go ahead, saying it would be held in January, and shuttled off to Brussels again – then back home to offer increasingly unconvincing assurances to her Eurosceptics about how and when we might exit the backstop. When the vote eventually came before the House on Wednesday 16 January it met with a record defeat for a sitting Prime Minister, of 230 votes – much larger than expected. Some Conservative remainers also voted against the deal. At that Tuesday night meeting before the vote, the ERG was in absolute consensus that the deal was hopeless and should be voted down.

But here's the problem. The ERG believed that it had time on its side. The UK was due to leave the European Union, by law, on 29 March 2019: in other words, it appeared to the Brexiteers that the choice would therefore either be May's deal or – the much better option – no deal at all, the default position. I can just about see how they could have thought that in December 2018. Just about. But by the beginning of 2019 that possibility surely no longer existed. From then on it was a case of either May's deal, a much, much softer deal relying on the support of the Labour Party, or no Brexit at all. The no-deal option was off the table – and it was by then clear that it was off the table because the House of Commons, with its vast remainer majority and its huge consensus that no deal was unacceptable, simply wouldn't let it happen. And yet during this time I spoke to plenty of Brexiteer MPs who would not or could not grasp this point. 'We have to leave – that's the law,' they would tell me, implacably. 'By what process could this possibly happen?' I would ask, and no salient answer was ever forthcoming. They somehow thought that Theresa May's 'running down the clock' played in their favour. But it didn't. It played directly into the hands of those who did not want Brexit at all. The ERGrs presumably believed that Brussels would cave in, given that the EU feared a no deal even more than the staunchest of UK remainers, and cede to their wishes regarding the backstop. But it has shown no inclination to do so. Or, they simply thought the only deal worth having is no deal at all – but that was an impossibility.

In December 2018 Dominic Grieve, the former Shadow Attorney General and a passionate remainer, tabled an amendment that eventually scotched any possibility of no deal going through, by transferring the power of decision regarding what must happen with Brexit from the executive to parliament. Given the weight of numbers in the House against Brexit, never mind no deal, it was clear from that moment on that no deal was not a possible outcome. How could the ERG not grasp this? The day after Theresa May lost her second meaningful vote, on 12 March, the House of Commons finally passed a motion preventing the UK from leaving the EU with no deal. And yet even after that I still heard Brexiteers (and some baleful remainers) insisting that no deal could still happen. How? By what possible mechanism?

The ERG was wrong-footed and misled by the Prime Minister time and again. The running down of the clock was not really a warning to the House that it's 'my deal or no deal': that was an empty slogan. It was a warning to the ERG that it was 'my deal or something much, much worse'. And that's what happened. Article 50 was extended by a gleeful Brussels and Theresa May announced talks with Jeremy Corbyn and his team on the construction of a deal to leave, which would not be leaving really in any shape or form. In defence, one ERG officer told me: 'I knew what was going on. I know [Brexit] is not going to happen. She was completely fucking mendacious. We made the mistake of taking her in good faith. All she did, when we talked to her, was blame Parliament.'

But if you knew, why not support her deal, even if it was a 'bucket of shit', as another member of the ERG put it to me? It was the best you could possibly get, given the circumstances – and might have been alterable somewhere down the line. But now there is talk that any deal will be 'locked' so that a more Eurosceptic Conservative Party, under a new leader, cannot alter the substance of it.

Theresa May's deal was a betrayal, for sure. I understand the views of those who say we would be better off staying in the EU than signing up to her fudge. But I rather agreed with Tom Harris, the former Scottish Labour Party politician and now a columnist at the *Daily Telegraph*. His point was this, broadly: 'Look, I have got slightly more than 50 per cent of what I voted for during that referendum. Given the result of the referendum that seems fair enough.' And that's why I think the ERG got it wrong in continually voting down her deal. No, it's not Brexit. But it's as good as you're likely to get and maybe once we're out we might reshape the whole thing. I thought that for a while, without being terribly convinced.

Concurrent to all this was the debate over Theresa May's leadership, and so we had the repeated non sequitur of May promising to stand down if the MPs would just vote for her stupid bloody deal. She was, it has to be said, an unpopular leader, within Parliament (although less so in the country). But the cynical conflation of those two issues was another reminder to the public that their wishes were not being acted upon, that they were subordinate to the future of the Conservative Party.

13

LOOK AT THE WOMAN
In those days before she finally departed . . .

You look at her. Standing at the dispatch box. Or upon returning from another hammering in Brussels, standing before the cameras in the stolen air of another dead evening. In the smart two-piece, before the cameras or before the dispatch box. Standing with that look on her face, the look she always has, of perturbed imperturbability. The voice hoarse and fading. Standing in front of the cameras or before the dispatch box, in the two-piece. Ashen and wretched and surely, by now, utterly exhausted, exhausted beyond endurance. Beaten down. Taking the questions, from Barnier and Tusk, or Corbyn and Rees-Mogg, or Ken Clarke and Anna Soubry, or Kuenssberg, or Maitlis. Ashen and wretched, the voice hoarse, the voice disappearing, the voice almost gone – standing there in her two-piece in front of everyone, with that look on her face. Reviled from every side at home. Reviled by her own party. Reviled by the furious Brexiteer MPs and her own activists for her betrayal. Reviled by the Tory remainers for her attempted compromises. Reviled or simply derided by the MPs from all the other parties, reviled or derided by the press. The worst Prime Minister in a hundred years. The most useless creature who ever walked the earth. And as soon as she is finished, yet again, the early alarm call and off to Brussels, to be held in contempt, to be almost pitied, to be discounted by the bemused or sniggering Europeans, her days, they know, numbered. And then back home, to be reviled again, this time with even more odium, even more contempt. The dead air in the ministerial limo as it curves along the M4 towards Heathrow. The migraine whine of the jet aeroplane. The once unctuous but now increasingly distant spads and civil servants beside her, not knowing where to look. The dead air in the ministerial limo back from the European parliament to Leopoldlaan and the airport, the migraine whine of the jet aeroplane. The ministerial limo curving along the M4. Back home terribly late and next day up bright and early to stand there in her two-piece, ashen, wretched, the voice hoarse. To be beaten. Beaten at every turn, defeat after defeat after defeat after defeat after defeat after defeat. And still standing there with that familiar look on her face, the look of perturbed imperturbability, the voice hoarse, the voice disappearing, the voice almost gone, standing there at the dispatch box ashen and wretched. And exhausted. Surely. Surely exhausted beyond endurance. Finally pleading with her own party, her allies, her friends, her colleagues, that she will give them what they want if they just come together for one supportive vote.

And what is it that they want, more than anything else? Her to go – to stand down, to piss off. We want nothing more than the end of you, Prime Minister, they tell her. Begone! And they tell her this as she stands before them, croaking and wan and exhausted, in her two-piece, beaten down. And in one final act of self-abnegation, she offers them this. I will go. Just vote this once. Just do that, and I'll be gone. Except it isn't quite a final act of self-abnegation, because – here's the thing – she has to do it again. And then again. And after that, they make her do it once more, to prostrate and humiliate herself. And even then they still won't vote for her deal, no matter how much they want her gone. Defeat after defeat after defeat after defeat. And she's still standing there in the two-piece with that familiar look on her face. And the voice even hoarser now. And her face ashen to the point of an almost occult luminosity. And so wretched. And surely so exhausted.

Why would she do it? And what sort of toll does that kind of stuff take on a human being? The mental toll, the physical toll, the human toll. Upon one woman. You surely cannot watch her, day after day, climbing back after each hammering and not feel sympathy. Is she doing it, as she says, for the good of the country? For the good of her party? Because she cannot think of anything else to do? In a sense, in a human sense, it does not much matter. Simply to say that it is a harrowing spectacle, an awful thing to behold, the woman with her ashen face, exhausted, with her ashen face and the voice almost gone. She has made mistakes, for sure. She has made mistakes and she keeps on making them. But she should not have to endure this, and nor should we. Perhaps she's OK. Perhaps she doesn't mind. But I don't think so. I don't think it's possible to not mind that stuff, the relentlessness of it, the defeat after defeat after defeat after defeat. And you look at the woman. And you wonder: have we done this? To her? Somehow?

* * *

Finally, she went – the voice breaking, the tears forming, in her two-piece, the face ashen, in front of the cameras, one last humiliation before the public. Thank Christ! Begone! And yet nothing material has changed, nor will change, because the maths is the same as it was before. No deal is still off the table, the remainers still control the House of Commons and have made that much abundantly clear. So what do we possess, then, in order to renegotiate with Brussels? Within minutes twelve potential leaders had declared themselves, the same ol same ol – Gove, Hunt, Johnson, Leadsom plus a whole bunch of chancers you've never heard of including James Cleverley who cleverly positioned himself as the kind of youthful change candidate and then equally cleverly withdrew when it transpired that even members of his own family wouldn't vote for him. Such vaulting ambition among these people who have let us down, ambition and an epic sense of entitlement. But nothing really changes with Theresa May's departure. Only, on a personal note, the hope that the image of her standing there before us, defeated and defeated and defeated, will sometime soon fade from my memory. No matter how hapless she was, or how conniving, nobody deserved THAT.

14

LABOUR AND BREXIT

I am against it because I believe the European Union to be a capitalist club that its problem is, it's for the few not the many. It uses free trade to take advantage of those that are in eastern Europe, Poles, Romanians who come over for a better life! Our wages are undercut because the Bosses think, because of the European Union they can pay them less! This is a complete and utter farce, we must work to actually improve our Nation for all of the people in this country.

David Mallon, Blyth Constituency
Labour Party delegate

The Labour Party's divisions over Brexit are more acute, mysterious and tortuous than even those of the Conservative Party. Look for a moment at the maths.

- Some 64 per cent of all parliamentary constituencies showed a majority for leave. Breaking this down still

further, somewhere between 60 per cent and 70 per cent
of Labour MPs represent constituencies that voted
leave. It is difficult to be more exact than this because
the vote for the referendum was not held on a constituency basis. Further, at least seventy-two Labour MPs
represent constituencies that voted leave by a considerable margin (i.e. above 55 per cent in favour of Brexit).

- But, 218 Labour MPs are believed to have voted remain
during the referendum, with only eleven voting leave.
To state the bleeding obvious for a moment, this shows
an enormous mismatch between what Labour MPs
wanted and what their benighted voters wanted.

- However, Labour Party members – the activists – are
overwhelmingly for remain. Some 88 per cent would
vote remain if a referendum was held again and 72 per
cent wish for a second vote because they didn't like
the result of the first one, according to a poll carried
out by Professor Tim Bale from Queen Mary
University of London in February 2019.

But the divisions then become even more complex.
Those Labour MPs who were either in favour of Brexit or
were, in public, more or less ambivalent about it are also
split into three distinct camps. There are those such as Kate
Hoey, Frank Field, John Mann and Gisela Stuart, largely
from what we might call the Blue Labour tendency: right of
centre on social issues and concerned about the UK's loss
of sovereignty in the European Union. Back when the UK
voted to remain within the EEC in 1975, this tranche would
have been represented by the likes of Peter Shore, a staunch

opponent of our involvement in Europe and about as far to the right as it is possible to get while still being a member of the Labour Party.

But then there is the old hard – more or less Marxist – left of the party, which sees the EU as the supranational entrenchment of capitalism, objects to the free movement of labour and capital (the means by which the rich get richer, according to Marx) and is perhaps also averse to the EU as a consequence of old cold war attitudinising, where everything the west did was to be opposed, from the Marshall Plan all the way through to the Maastricht Treaty. It is true that by and large the further right you travel in politics, the more likely you are to be in favour of Brexit. But it is also true that the further to the left you travel, the more you will be in favour of Brexit. Virtually all of the deranged far-left UK fringe parties with the word 'Communist' somewhere in their titles were pro-Brexit, as was the Socialist Workers Party.

It came as something of a shock, then, to the youthful, wildly pro-EU Momentum members who joined in a flood in 2015 and elevated Jeremy Corbyn to the unlikely position of leader of the party that their hero had been and perhaps still was an implacable opponent of a European superstate. Corbyn had been with the hard left in 1975 and voted against Britain's membership of the EEC. He was still with the hard left in 1992 and opposed to the signing of the Maastricht Treaty. He said at the time:

the whole basis of the Maastricht treaty is the establishment of a European central bank which is staffed by

bankers, independent of national Governments and national economic policies, and whose sole policy is the maintenance of price stability[.] That will undermine any social objective that any Labour Government in the United Kingdom – or any other Government – would wish to carry out . . . The Maastricht treaty does not take us in the direction of the checks and balances contained in the American federal constitution[.] It takes us in the opposite direction of an unelected legislative body – the Commission – and, in the case of foreign policy, a policy Commission that will be, in effect, imposing foreign policy on nation states that have fought for their own democratic accountability.

Well, indeed. And given that Mr Corbyn has not changed his views on anything else in the last forty years one should probably assume he thinks exactly the same thing right now. There's plenty of evidence for such a conclusion. Much more recently, Corbyn had also voted against the EU's Lisbon Treaty and supported a referendum on Britain's exit from the EU. In 2009 he attacked the EU as a 'European Empire of the 21st Century' and a 'military Frankenstein' (I am not entirely sure what he meant by that). Later he castigated the EU for its 'bullying' of socialist Greece. This takes us up to Corbyn's state of mind, 2011.

The problem for Corbyn, though, and his likeminded cabal at the top of the party, was that Labour in parliament was heavily pro-remain, especially among the vast numbers of dispossessed Blairites who had seen their party taken away from them. And while on some issues, such as nationalisation and increased taxes, Corbyn could drive through a hard left agenda with the jubilant support of the party activists, the young Momentum hordes who now had control of the party apparatus, he found this much more difficult when it came to the EU, because his supporter base was hugely in favour of it. Thus Corbyn shifted his position a little; he made an accommodation. There was an 'over-whelming' case for staying in the EU, he announced, having given the EU a mark of seven and a half out of ten. And, without very much enthusiasm, he campaigned for remain in a singularly lukewarm manner, as far as his despairing backbench Blairite MPs were concerned.

So, by mid-July 2016 we had something of a paradox on our hands. A Prime Minister who believed we should remain in the EU leading negotiations to take us out of it, facing a leader of the opposition who almost certainly believed we should get the hell out but was constrained by the fervent objections to this position from his own party in parliament and indeed his own supporters.

Corbyn was not the only far-leftie to perform a swift volte face. His chief supporter in the British press, Owen Jones – known at the *Guardian* as 'Squealer', the fat pig who acts as Minister for Propaganda in George Orwell's book, *Animal Farm* – did likewise, in a similarly short period of time. As the former Labour MP Denis MacShane (a committed remainer) notes in his forthcoming book *Brexiternity*:

A year before the referendum Owen Jones, the news-paper columnist who today has the most influence on the left in Britain, urged his *Guardian* readers to support what he called Lexit – a left-wing exit from the EU. Jones condemned the EU in language that was common to members of the Campaign Group of Labour MPs, the hard left-wing block of MPs who carried the torch for Tony Benn's 1970s and early 1980s hostility to Europe that inspired Jeremy Corbyn and his No 2, the Labour shadow chancellor, John McDonnell. Jones proclaimed that EU 'treaties and directives enforce free market policies based in privatisation and marketization of our public services and utilities.'

Two years later, though, this yapping clown was calling for a second referendum.

I mentioned that the leavers within the Parliamentary Labour Party were split three ways – and so far I've mentioned the old hard left and the pro-working class right. The third group consists of about twelve MPs who have been pressing the leadership for what we might call a harder Brexit. This little gang includes the admirable Caroline Flint, a former Blairite who voted remain in the referendum but wishes that the aspirations of her electorate (in Doncaster) be respected. Eleven of the twelve MPs represent constituencies where the leave vote exceeded 60 per cent, so you can make your own judgement as to whether they are motivated by principle or by an overwhelming desire to save their seats. In either case, they're OK by me.

So – Labour's quandary is that it is led by a cabal that is still most likely in favour of Brexit, constrained by a

Parliamentary Labour Party that is overwhelmingly in favour of remain, activists who are overwhelmingly in favour of remain and a voter base that preferred to leave. A split in the party (and among voters) on political lines but also a split in terms of north versus south, London versus the rest, young versus old, middle class versus working class. A division, then, not dissimilar to that which afflicted the entire country. And so given this problematic divide, you can easily understand why Labour's official position on Brexit has been one of fence sitting, prevarication and obfuscation. There have been basically four guiding principles, one of which is simply opportunistic and two of which seem to be contradictory to one another.

The Shadow Brexit Secretary, Keir Starmer, a capable politician, was quick to insist that the referendum result did not imply an exit from the European Union's Customs Union and that a hard Brexit, with no deal, would be injurious to the country (and most importantly to jobs). How Sir Keir reached his first conclusion I'm not sure: the vote seems to me to imply precisely that we must leave the Customs Union, as it is one of the pillars of the very thing from which we voted to escape. But Sir Keir is a lawyer and I'm not. Either way, Labour has stuck to its insistence that we should not leave the Customs Union and that 'no deal' is off the table.

The party has also abided by a commitment to respect the result of the referendum, a statement to which effect is included in the party's manifesto. My view is that this contradicts Starmer's insistence upon remaining within the Customs Union, for obvious reasons. More to the point, 'respecting the result of the referendum' has become a meaningless platitude. There is nobody who doesn't respect the result of the referendum. Even Michael Heseltine respects the result of the referendum – he just thinks it should be ignored. Respected and ignored. Others trot out the same line but add that, for the sake of democracy, they simply want another one, or insist that the referendum wasn't binding, or didn't mean what it said it meant and so on.

Still, there was no appetite among the Labour leadership for a second referendum, which forms the third consistent party policy on Brexit. And this despite the demands for such from within the Parliamentary Labour Party and from Labour commentators (yes, including the hapless Owen Jones) in the daily papers. The pressure was continually on Corbyn to make Labour the 'party of remain': in the *Guardian*, *The Times*, the *Independent*, from large swathes of his own parliamentary party and indeed his own fanbase. That he did not do so is to his credit, regardless of the practical consequences of reneging on a manifesto commitment and ostracising the millions of Labour voters who voted leave and wished their decision to be put into effect.

The final principle was purely pragmatic: to cause as many problems for the Prime Minister as was humanly possible, especially after her position had been fatally weakened by the 2017 general election, with the hope of securing a vote of no confidence and a general election. And its paradoxical counterpart – to keep Theresa May as leader of the Conservative Party. There is a facile truism that oppositions are meant to oppose: Labour did this cleverly. While rejecting a second referendum and standing by its commit-ment to honour the vote of 2016, Starmer and Corbyn continually made conditions for voting in favour of a deal that were so at odds with the meaning of 'leave' that even Theresa May could not agree to them. Of course, they did not intend her to agree with them. These demands were first made in the form of 'six tests' to be applied to any deal, stipulations so vague as to be almost meaningless, and deliberately so:

1. Does it ensure a strong and collaborative future rela-tionship with the EU?
2. Does it deliver the 'exact same benefits' as we currently have as members of the Single Market and Customs Union?
3. Does it ensure the fair management of migration in the interests of the economy and communities?
4. Does it defend rights and protections and prevent a race to the bottom?
5. Does it protect national security and our capacity to tackle cross-border crime?
6. Does it deliver for all regions and nations of the UK?

The exact same benefits? How would that be possible, if we were to leave? And what is meant by 'fair management of migration'? And who is proposing a 'race to the bottom' and what the hell does it mean? Does it deliver *what* for all regions and nations of the UK? It is worth saying here that one of the principal Lexit arguments – the exploitation of foreign labour and the consequent undercutting of domestic wages – had somehow lost its allure for the far left. Somehow they conflated the issue of immigration with racism and thus, being fervently against the latter, found themselves required to speak in support of the former.

Anyway, there was no deal Theresa May could come up with that would satisfy these ectoplasmic criteria, and if she did come up with one then I have little doubt that Labour would have swiftly changed the criteria.

When, eventually, the Prime Minister was forced to open talks with Labour in the hope of getting a butchered version of her hopeless deal through Parliament, those six tests boiled down to a demand to stay in the Customs Union (i.e. not leaving the EU) and preserved rights for workers and EU nationals living in the UK. And still, behind the arras, the Blairites were demanding another stipulation be a second referendum, a cry increasingly taken up in Brussels.

The Labour leadership, whatever grave faults they may possess with regard to other matters (and which are too numerous to detail here), are not, however, the primary villains of this piece. For sure, Labour has been disingenuous, evasive, shifting and vague. Further, the leadership was happy to leave Theresa May hanging for party political reasons, rather than both respect the decision the people of this country had taken and work for the national good in fashioning a deal that did respect that vote, for the good of the country. They played their part, then, in scuppering Brexit for good and all. And the vast tranche of Labour MPs who demanded the vote be ignored or a second vote taken deserve a goodly share of bile and opprobrium. But loathsome though the party has become, latterly, they were not the main architects of Brexit's demise. That title rests with Theresa May, the government and parliament.

If there's an upside to this farrago, it's that Labour's prevarications have led to catastrophe in the polling booths. The May Euro elections saw them eclipsed by a resurgent Liberal Democratic Party – and nor was that a one-off. They retained the seat of Peterborough only very narrowly (with a candidate who 'liked' anti-Semitic posts) having organised a copious postal-vote campaign primarily among the city's Pakistani community.

15

BACKSTOP

The Northern Ireland 'backstop' is a kind of insurance policy to keep 'frictionless' trade on the 310-mile border between Northern Ireland, part of the UK, and the Republic of Ireland, which is of course in the European Union. For reasons occasioned by British governmental ineptitude, pig ignorance and duplicity, as well as Irish and EU spite and intractability, it somehow became the biggest stumbling block to a trade deal between Britain and the EU, the thing that stopped Brexit.

This should never have been allowed to happen. There were always going to be problems extricating ourselves from the EU, but this really should not have been one of them. Put simply, perhaps too simply, the Irish did not want a 'hard' border with the UK, and the UK did not want a hard border with Ireland – so, in other words, if there were to be a hard border it would be imposed by the EU against the will of both sovereign states. The backstop issue was further complicated by the result of the 2017 general election, in which Theresa May found her government dependent on the ten votes of the Democratic Unionist Party for her survival in office, all of whom were adamant (reasonably enough) that Brexit should apply equally across the whole of the UK and that Northern Ireland should not be a special case, a kind of halfway house between being independent and being an EU satrapy. Perhaps the issue also lost May her majority, for in her earlier dealings with Brussels she had signed up to a deal that aligned Northern Ireland with the EU and thus separated it from the rest of the UK, which is clearly wrong.

Later she attempted to ameliorate this position by saying that for a temporary period, at least, the whole of the UK would effectively remain within the EU's Customs Union. That's not what we voted for, either. Either way, the deal May kept putting before the increasingly weary House of Commons tied the UK to a backstop over which we had no jurisdiction and that left us effectively members of the Customs Union and subject to various other EU institutions either temporarily or in perpetuity.

It is certainly true that the Irish recognised the Northern Ireland problem long before the British did. Brexit scared the republic, and with probable good reason. The UK is easily Ireland's biggest trading partner, with imports and exports amounting to about £30 billion per year. And so, as Rory Carroll and Lisa O'Carroll wrote for the *Guardian*: 'Enda Kenny, the then taoiseach, ordered the first Brexit impact study in 2014. Officials identified the impact on the economy, diplomatic ties, and crucially the Good Friday agreement and what Brexit would mean for the border. A further 85-page report was produced in November 2015 outlining consequences of a yes and a no vote.'

Once the leave vote had been secured in the UK, the Irish – with a new Taoiseach in Leo Varadkar – went into overdrive. They strove to build a consensus among the twenty-six other European Union states to ensure that whatever happened in the forthcoming Brexit negotiations, Ireland was not to be left in the position of having a hard border with the north of the island. They were eminently successful in securing that consensus. Varadkar was canny, if disingenuous. At every stage he insisted that provision for a soft border was not primarily about trade, but was essential to keep the peace enshrined in the 1998 Good Friday Agreement. The asinine non sequitur – supported by some remainers over here, such as John Major and Tony Blair – being that customs checks on goods travelling between north and south might somehow reignite the Troubles. It is a ludicrous hypothesis. The British had never envisaged border checkpoints with barbed wire, landmines and British soldiers armed with machine guns. Nor was there the slightest suspicion that we would need to return to that state. Why would we? Nor, further, is there anything in the Good Friday Agreement that directly ties the United Kingdom to the European Union, even if frictionless trade between the UK and Ireland was taken as a given when the document was signed.

The primary job of a government is to look after its country's interests, so it is perhaps otiose to blame the oily little shit Varadkar for his continued intransigence over the issue. But it is true, too, that the nastier Varadkar became to the British, the higher rose his opinion poll ratings. And some (not me, as it happens) suspected that his endgame was not merely to humiliate the British while protecting his country's interests, but also to navigate towards a position where a united Ireland was once again on the agenda, given that the majority of Ulstermen had voted remain. Either way, Varadkar's posturing and his intractability seemed to lack the sort of good faith one hopes to find between neighbours. What do I mean by good faith between neighbours? A mindfulness of each other's aspirations and needs, a certain amicability. The kind of amicability that persuaded the UK to loan Ireland £3.2 billion, on very favourable terms, when the country's basket-case economy finally went bankrupt in 2010 and its banks began to implode. That kind of good faith. Ireland also needed financial assistance from the International Monetary Fund, the European Commission and the hopeless European Central Bank, so parlous was its position. Ireland has been paying back the loan and is due to continue doing so until 2021. If I were the Chancellor of the Exchequer, I'd ratchet up the interest rate a little higher, you know?

But Varadkar is not the principal villain of this piece: that would be, as ever, our own government. Its failure to sequence negotiations properly (so that the backstop crisis became inevitable), its lack of wit and its mindless ineffectuality over the issue. As the pro-Brexit writer Alastair Dow put it: 'It is one thing for the EU and Ireland to have made their bad faith and the unnecessary, draconian nature of their agreement so clear. It is quite another for the UK

Government to have let this happen in the first place, and to have put itself in a position where it is both unprepared and unable to stand up for itself, tear up the Agreement, leave without one and negotiate a new trade deal from a position of strength.'

We were too slow to understand the depth of Ireland's hostility, too slow to demolish the absurd injunction that a few customs checks here and there might lead to the IRA bombing people again. Varadkar's narrative fitted very neatly with the remainer narrative and that of the EU: this isn't about trade, it is about peace between nations, the whole reason the European Community was founded in the first place, all those years ago. This specious rot was never properly challenged by the British until it was way too late.

But there was worse: crimes of neglect, of ignorance, of a failure to engage. Many, perhaps all, of the problems associated with the Irish border could have been circumvented by technology. Borders today are not so much geographical as rooted in time. The movement of goods and people does not need to be physically checked at the point of entry: there are a multitude of ways around the problem. But the government seemed either uninterested in them or utterly ignorant of them. Blockchain technology, for example, is used to keep a record of transactions in various crypto-currencies, but is increasingly deployed by big companies to keep track of goods travelling to and fro. The ports of both Houston and Rotterdam, for example, are equipped with the blockchain technology to enable speedy and efficient processing of goods, following a joint venture between the maritime shipping firm Maersk and IBM. What did the government know about blockchain? Trixy Sanderson, who worked for a company developing the system, had meetings with MPs from select committees who, she reported, were utterly unaware of the latest development, of what could be done, and did not remotely understand the technology. Asked about the problem of border relations with Ireland, the Chancellor of the Exchequer, Philip Hammond, said: 'There is technology becoming available . . . I don't claim to be an expert on it but the most obvious is blockchain.' The insouciance and the ineptitude amaze. Why aren't you an expert on it, Phil? Is there nobody in your department who is an expert on blockchain? Have you not asked someone to maybe investigate the business a little? Blockchain, or an alternative method of registering the movement of goods across frontiers utilising satellites, is with us right now. It would cost a bit of money to get a process up and running, without doubt, but as Stephen Pope, writing for *Forbes* in October 2018, put it:

> Critics may well claim that the time, cost and sheer scale of building and implementing a customs system based on blockchain would be long and expensive. They will also point to the shifting sands of EU and UK politics in that what may be agreed to in 2019 could be undermined by a series of political changes in the EU and UK over the next five-years. That is so short-sighted as this technology can offer a smooth solution to the issue of identifying products that would come into the EU via the UK to ensure compliance with EU regulatory standards.

Indeed, as Pope suggests in his opening sentence, plenty of people have pointed out that the technology is too distant for it to be of immediate use (it isn't) and that it is not the answer to all of the problems posed by the Irish border (no, just almost all). They are usually remainers. Both Leo Varadkar and the EU negotiating team stuck fast to the notion that technology would not solve the Irish question, it could only be solved by the UK ceding ground and agreeing, in effect, to a customs union with the EU. This was, of course, a convenient line for them to hold as it placed the pressure on the UK – and held it was until the spring of 2019, when Varadkar suddenly admitted that technology (basically blockchain) could solve almost all of the problems surrounding this 'backstop' business, except for maybe the transportation of livestock. Brussels agreed – but the UK was still miles behind the curve.

Varadkar's admission is important, although the truth of what he said was evident three years ago, as soon as we voted to leave the European Union – it's just that the UK government never grasped the point. There is the technology available to bypass almost all of the problems occasioned by the Irish border. Meanwhile, the checking of livestock could be done not at the border point, but at the farms within both the republic and Northern Ireland. A minor hassle, I think, but necessary to stop the poor Irish people being flooded with tons of evil mutant chlorinated chickens, which is what seems to have been worrying Varadkar (and indeed the anti-US lobby over here). Is it a hassle of sufficient gravity that it will convince Seamus O'Semtex and his merry friends of the pressing need to start bombing Protestants once again? I have my doubts, you know, even if the IRA's expansive smuggling operations make it averse to borders of any kind. Meanwhile, Irish people would also be required to show their passports when they entered the north – just as we must show our passports when we enter, uh, Ireland, right now. Have you ever travelled to France or Austria without a passport? Is it any different from trying to get into Switzerland, Norway, Canada or, for that matter, Serbia?

The backstop. The bloody backstop. It was ever a chimera, a confected mess of an issue, used cleverly by both the EU and Irish government to blackmail the leaver Brits. And it worked. You have to say that – it worked.

16

AND NOW?

Betcha we don't leave. I think most leave voters had the same suspicion, the same inkling, three years ago, even before all the shrieking began, before David Lammy and Anna Soubry et al. insisted we ignore the vote entirely, mid-morning of 24 June. The interesting thing was 'how' we wouldn't leave. Simple maths, I suppose. Not the maths of 17.4 million versus 16.1 million, or 52 per cent versus 48. The other maths, the cleverer maths. If you control parliament and the broadcast media you will likely get your way, you will control the narrative. A narrative that somehow towards the end, rather magnificently, portrayed those who actually wished to leave the EU as 'extremist' and 'intransigent', a twisting of the truth exactly 180 degrees. In Britain, peasants' revolts never end up terribly well, for the peasants – and so it has turned out this time, much as it did in 1381. Everybody who had power (if not hegemony) was against Brexit. That was the maths that counted. Yes, there was ineptitude of a sometimes hilarious measure, but it was in the balance of power that the thing was decided. A betrayal, for sure, and one that is corrosive for our democracy and humiliating for the country.

And I suppose that what we do now in the short term is wander down to the polls and maybe vote for Nigel Farage's Brexit Party (with a scented handkerchief held to our noses, in many cases) and curse to damnation the two major parties. After that? A new Conservative Party leader – but the same division in the House of Commons and within the party itself. A general election perhaps – in which the same parties, staffed by the same people, have all the weight, money and influence and will thus end up getting all the seats. Assuming people are even minded to turn out and vote. *What is the point?* many leave voters will be asking themselves. *We did vote. And look what happened.* That is what I hear in my home town, in Middlesbrough, all the time. What is the point?

Brexit was a singularity, for sure. Never have so many people voted, never has their decision been so blatantly gainsaid. And in that singularity it has perhaps done us all a service, because it has laid bare divisions within our society that run a lot deeper than simply an argument over the usefulness of the European Union. As I've pointed out many times in this book, perhaps too many, the public voted by a smallish majority to leave the EU. But in the House of Commons every major party had a majority of MPs in favour of remaining, except for the DUP. Leave-minded MPs were outnumbered by about six to one. The House of Commons was, therefore, grossly unrepresentative of the people. If Brexit had been an anomaly, a one-off issue that uniquely cut across party lines, then perhaps we could put it down to experience and move on. But of course, it is not.

There is a vast tranche of voters in this country whose views are simply unrepresented, full stop. They are the voters who are not liberals, in the modern sense of the term. They have an affection for the nation state, for their own communities and for the traditions and history of our nation. Many still cleave to the notion that we are primarily a Christian country and may be worried about the challenge posed by Islam. They are averse to uncontrolled immigration – most opinion polls put the figure at about 70–80 per cent who wish immigration reduced, a good 40 per cent want it stopped altogether and more than half think large-scale immigration has not been beneficial to the country. Averse to uncontrolled immigration, then, but not part of that 3 or 4 per cent who are proudly racist.

These are also the voters who are wearied beyond measure of the shrieked complaints from the ever-growing hierarchies of acquired victimhood. They are not homophobic, but may have doubts about gay adoptions (a majority of the country, according to the last British social attitudes survey) and are probably bemused and appalled when their children are taught about the wonders of transgenderism in junior school. They believe in marriage, and the longevity of marriage and the notion of 'doing the right thing'. But, by the same token, they are worried by the growing gap between rich and poor, between London and the south-east of the country, and have no great problem with more equitable taxation and nationalisation. They regret the passing of the notion of freedom of speech. How do we know these people exist, in large numbers? The social research surveys and opinion polls tell us, is how. But the House of Commons does not remotely reflect their views. Until February 2019, of the nine parties represented in the House of Commons, eight signed up to the full liberal agenda (the exception again being the ten MPs of the DUP). Then a new party was formed – Change UK – who were revealed to be even more liberal than the others. So, of ten parties in the House, nine are liberal even if one is called Conservative. (It is the Conservative Party that has decided not to bother tackling immigration and the Conservative Party that insists schoolkids as young as six must be taught about same-sex relationships and trans-genderism. And of course it is the Conservative MPs, by a majority, whose disdain for the nation state compelled them to vote remain.)

Who do they vote for, these unrepresented people? Well, speaking as one of them, I continued to vote Labour, despite loathing the party's infantile far-left agitprop, visceral anti-Semitism and apparent contempt for everything about this country. Many others tribally do so despite – as we know from the polls – being averse to much of what modern Labour stands for. (Nor, incidentally, were we all convinced by Tony Blair: a liberal, again.) Some migrated to UKIP for a while, many of whom will not have liked that party's Thatcherite economic policies. Many vote Conservative, while wishing it were a little more . . . conservative. Some may even have voted Lib Dem, as a protest vote. Whatever, this tranche of opinion – somewhere between 30 and 45 per cent of the electorate, at a conservative estimate – simply has no representation any more. Brexit pretty much proved that. The only party that broadly represents the mindset I outlined above is the Social Democratic Party, of which I'm now a member. But we're small in size, if rapidly growing.

Who are they, these lost voters? A very diverse bunch. The northern working class, many people from BME communities who appreciate support for both the family and their religious faith, One Nation Tories, the elderly – but increasing numbers of young people too – the affluent, the poor, the left behind, the go-ahead. They are not a homogenous bunch, then. Almost the only thing they have in common is an aversion to liberal social policies and neoliberal economic and foreign policies. The left–right axis does not apply any more: these are people who may well agree with a few of John McDonnell's economic strategies and yet find themselves in concurrence with Jacob Rees-Mogg on many social issues. The same sort of voters who, in the USA, transferred their votes from the socialist Bernie Sanders straight into the lap of Donald Trump. Anyone but the liberal!

You can see the revolt against liberalism in the USA, then – but also in Europe and beyond. The rapid growth of populist parties from both right and left has shattered the old Christian Democrat vs Social Democrat duopoly from Thessaloniki to Gothenburg, Naples to Warsaw. Italy's coalition government is shared between the right-wing populist Northern League and the leftish populist Five Star. Populists now either rule or partially rule most of the Visegrád countries and recently deprived the Dutch Prime

Minister, Mark Rutte, of his majority. In almost every country within the EU, the liberals are on the run. It has become
a (rightly) discredited creed, associated with an influx of
immigrants, a progressive culture that is largely not wanted,
financial austerity and a foreign policy that has led to
bloody and disastrous interventions in the Middle East,
subsequent civil wars and rise of the Islamic State. The
invasion of Iraq was in many way the quintessential expression of modern liberalism; hopelessly misguided (and
illegal) but powered also by that peculiar brand of overweening arrogance – the mistaken notion that everybody
wants the same thing, that we are at the end of history and
that, with the dutiful application of a few million tons of
high-explosive ordnance, people might be bombed into
being consensual, liberal, free-market democrats. It did not
work in Iraq and it does not work anywhere else and history
is far from being at an end. The things the liberals think are
'sorted' are not remotely so, even if opposition to each
mistaken shibboleth is often cowed into quiescence.

For the people of Europe are also discovering that the
liberal elite that presides over them, in the form of the EU's
institutions, is an extremely intolerant, bullying beast: it
cannot bear to be countermanded and doles out punish-
ments to countries that dare to stray from its dated and
otiose prescriptions.

So, the populists are on the march. And even in those
countries where they are not either part of the government,
or the entire government – at least they are represented in
parliament. We are one of the few EU countries to have a
first-past-the-post electoral system – and as all three of our

major parties have been captured by the liberal ideology, there is no room on either the government or opposition benches for those who beg to differ, with one exception. The Scottish National Party is also a populist party and its extraordinary success of late has been based upon offering electors north of the border a sense of place, history, tradition and belonging and an opposition to being ruled from afar. The SNP is well established in Scotland and now in parliament. For our own parliament to better represent the breadth of opinion south of the border, we need proportional representation. We need diversity of opinion in parliament.

The problem, though, is that it is not just parliament. The liberals also run the BBC, our universities, almost all government quangos, academia and the teaching profession and they are wonderfully illiberal when it comes to tolerating views that differ from their own. When someone from beyond the liberal consensus is appointed to a position of power – an occurrence that is so rare as to be counted on the fingers of one hand – they are quickly hounded out, as both Roger Scruton and Toby Young recently found to their cost. How on earth does one persuade the BBC to change? There have been countless studies that demand of the Corporation that it acknowledge its relentless liberal (not left-wing) bias (see Chapter 6), that it at the very least recognises that its journalists and producers inhabit an echo chamber in which everyone agrees with everybody else about everything – and yet the BBC does nothing whatsoever to address the issue. In the past ten years the Corporation has responded well to correct accusations that it was overwhelmingly white. Why can it not be forced to respond to equally accurate observations that it is also overwhelmingly middle class and politically homogenous? They all think the same, up there in New Broadcasting House. Just as they all think the same among the spires of Oxford and in the staff room of every London comprehensive school, on the boards of the arts quangos, in all of the institutions that govern our lives. They all think the same. And so, because everyone thinks pretty much the same way, they do not consider it political bias at all – they just think it's *right*. But beyond this pleasant metropolitan consensus, out there in that godforsaken, backwards, crippled hinterland of 'middle England', there is a great deal of dispute and disagreement. There are millions of people who are utterly averse to the policies inflicted upon them.

If any good is to come of this Brexit farrago, this humiliation, this betrayal – then it will be a realisation that this hyper- liberal elite is a very dangerous state of affairs for society. Dangerous and unjust. There are millions of people who feel disenfranchised – and indeed, have been disenfranchised – with no conduit for their opposition and anger. The Brexit referendum result itself was evidence that the political make-up of the House of Commons is not remotely reflective of the divide in society, and that the old left–right stuff (a throwback to the French Revolution, for God's sake) was, in the minds of the people, irrelevant. And if the referendum didn't teach the politicians that, then the Euro elections on 23 May 2019, in which the two main parties secured just one quarter of the vote between them, should have driven the message home. It is corrosive and hugely damaging to social cohesion to have a very large proportion of the population – in most cases the majority – deprived of a viewpoint, told that they are stupid and racist for wishing to leave the EU, stupid and racist for wishing for lower levels of immigration, stupid and racist for liking the idea of the nation state and possessing a pride in being British. Decrying people for being stupid and racist because they disagree with you doesn't do it any more, as a mode of political discourse. We have had it with being told to shut up and get with the programme. If the liberals will not accept civilised opposition to their fatuous agenda, then the worry is that the opposition will become very uncivilised. To an extent – with the growth of, for example, the English Defence League and Britain First – this is already happening. Brexit may simply have been the first skirmish in a war for Britain's soul. Unless the liberals shed a little bit of arrogance and certitude, it could become a very nasty war indeed.

* * *

Every book needs a hero, and this one is desperately short of them. So let me, late in the day, give you two heroes: a couple of people you most likely don't know. They are both friends of mine – Tim Wright and Jim Carter. Old school friends, actually – I've known Tim since I was thirteen and he's been my closest mate ever since. We bonded over weird music and pretentious literature back in Middlesbrough and tried to get high by smoking dried banana skins or eating tablespoons full of nutmeg. Didn't work. Tim got out of the Boro as soon as he could but still retains a rooted affection for the place. He works as a psychotherapist in London. Jim I knew only vaguely from school on account of the fact that we had both shagged the same rather aloof girl. By vaguely I mean I didn't even twig that he was Indian back in the day, so pale was his skin. Latterly we have become great friends and forty-five years after we briefly and uncomfortably met now enjoy getting pissed, every so often, in The Anchor pub, in Guisborough, the town where we both went to school. He's the top anaesthetist at the James Cook Hospital in Middlesbrough. Jim got out – but came back to Teesside. Enormously valued friends, then – but also heroes. They would both deny that they were, which is, I suppose, characteristic of heroes. Heroes usually have that self-deprecatory thing going on.

Both men voted in the 2016 referendum. Both men thought about it long and hard and maybe even agonised a bit. Both men voted remain. And both were dismayed, or disappointed, or aghast, when the result came through the next day. Shocked, discombobulated. And both men now regret the decision of the majority of the British people and wish it had been different. And both men now think that nonetheless that decision must – MUST – be upheld – no second referendum, no reneging, no weaselling out of it. And they think that because they respect democracy. They understand who won, in that vote. Not their side. The other side. And the process that has unfolded since 24 June 2016 disturbs them every bit as much as it disturbs those of us who voted to leave.

My guess is that this view is prevalent among the vast majority of remainers: a common decency that respects that other people have views that differ from their own and that those views should not be disregarded. When we talk about Brexit, they do not call me a Nazi, or a moron, or a xenophobe. We agree instead to differ. And so when people say that Brexit has led to a corrosive divide in the country, they are perhaps overstating the case. It is not a corrosive divide between the 17.4 million and the 16.1 million. It is a corrosive divide between that four to five million of remainers who are seemingly incapable of understanding that other people have views that differ from their own and that this might be for valid reasons, rather than because they are uneducated *Untermensch*. The four or five million who defriend people because they voted leave, who exist within one or another echo chamber – in the BBC, the civil service, academia, other parts of the largely public sector – where opposing views are so scarce as to be virtually invisible. It is true that a little more than this number signed a petition calling for another vote, but it is a very easy thing to click on a link. I'm referring to the hard core. The ones transfixed by apoplexy and who believe that democracy has maybe gone too far. You'll do something about it Mummy, you always do. How do we shed light on these remote, insulated corners of our society? How do we get the BBC and the universities and the quangos and the charities and the luvvees to embrace diversity of opinion as well as diversity of race and creed? It does not matter how often they are told that theirs is a minority opinion – and on most issues a very small minority opinion – they will not accept the fact. They are intractable, cocooned and oblivious and when challenged on their beliefs act with a totalitarian fury. Brexit at least showed us this, a picture of a country dominated by a hyper-liberal elite that has power without hegemony.

ARTICLE 50 OF THE TREATY ON EUROPEAN UNION

Article 50

1. Any Member State may decide to withdraw from the Union in accordance with its own constitutional requirements.

2. A Member State which decides to withdraw shall notify the European Council of its intention. In the light of the guidelines provided by the European Council, the Union shall negotiate and conclude an agreement with that State, setting out the arrangements for its withdrawal, taking account of the framework for its future relationship with the Union. That agreement shall be negotiated in accordance with Article 218(3) of the Treaty on the Functioning of the European Union. It shall be concluded on behalf of the Union by the Council, acting by a qualified majority, after obtaining the consent of the European Parliament.

3. The Treaties shall cease to apply to the State in question from the date of entry into force of the withdrawal agreement or, failing that, two years after the notification referred to in paragraph 2, unless the European Council, in agreement with the Member State concerned, unanimously decides to extend this period.

4. For the purposes of paragraphs 2 and 3, the member of the European Council or of the Council representing the withdrawing Member State shall not participate in the discussions of the European Council or Council or in decisions concerning it.

   A qualified majority shall be defined in accordance with Article 238(3)(b) of the Treaty on the Functioning of the European Union.

5. If a State which has withdrawn from the Union asks to rejoin, its request shall be subject to the procedure referred to in Article 49.

ACKNOWLEDGEMENTS

Most of the people who I should thank for their help with this book would very much prefer it if I did not disclose their names – cabinet ministers, former cabinet ministers, ERGrs, Labour MPs and so on. But thanks to them all the same. Nigel Farage had no such reservations, so thank you for your usual candour, Nigel. Thanks are also owed to Trixy Sanderson, journalist James Forsyth (the *Spectator*) and Matt Kelly (the *New European*) and the former Labour MP Denis MacShane. Facebook friends contributed anecdotes and suggestions – and conversations with comrades in the Social Democratic Party, leader William Clouston and Patrick O'Flynn, helped to form the narrative, much as did John Gray's coruscating analysis of hyper-liberalism. Thanks for their encouragement and help to my agent Eugenie Furniss and my editor at Little, Brown, Andreas Campomar. And as ever, thanks to my wife, Alicia Liddle, and my daughter, Emmeline Liddle, for their supreme patience.

Saltburn, June 2019